Developing Applications with Azure Active Directory

Principles of Authentication and Authorization for Architects and Developers

Manas Mayank
Mohit Garg

Apress®

Developing Applications with Azure Active Directory: Principles of Authentication and Authorization for Architects and Developers

Manas Mayank
Hyderabad, India

Mohit Garg
Hyderabad, India

ISBN-13 (pbk): 978-1-4842-5039-6
https://doi.org/10.1007/978-1-4842-5040-2

ISBN-13 (electronic): 978-1-4842-5040-2

Managing Director, Apress Media LLC: Welmoed Spahr
Acquisitions Editor: Smriti Srivastava
Development Editor: Siddhi Chavan
Coordinating Editor: Shrikant Vishwakarma

Cover designed by eStudioCalamar

Cover image designed by Freepik (www.freepik.com)

Distributed to the book trade worldwide by Springer Science+Business Media New York, 233 Spring Street, 6th Floor, New York, NY 10013. Phone 1-800-SPRINGER, fax (201) 348-4505, e-mail orders-ny@springer-sbm.com, or visit www.springeronline.com. Apress Media, LLC is a California LLC and the sole member (owner) is Springer Science + Business Media Finance Inc (SSBM Finance Inc). SSBM Finance Inc is a **Delaware** corporation.

For information on translations, please e-mail rights@apress.com, or visit http://www.apress.com/rights-permissions.

Apress titles may be purchased in bulk for academic, corporate, or promotional use. eBook versions and licenses are also available for most titles. For more information, reference our Print and eBook Bulk Sales web page at http://www.apress.com/bulk-sales.

Any source code or other supplementary material referenced by the author in this book is available to readers on GitHub via the book's product page, located at www.apress.com/978-1-4842-5039-6. For more detailed information, please visit http://www.apress.com/source-code.

Printed on acid-free paper

To my parents, Mrs. Ranjana Poddar and Mr. B.B. Poddar. No words could do justice to all that you have done.

To my sisters, Santwana Poddar and Anima Poddar, you both are the best that happened to me.

—Manas Mayank

This book is dedicated to my parents, Pawan Kumar Garg and Saroj Garg. Without their sacrifices, I wouldn't have accomplished whatever I have in my life.

I would also like to dedicate this to my wife, Samiksha Gupta, who is always standing by my side and supporting me during tough times.

—Mohit Garg

Table of Contents

About the Authors

Manas Mayank is currently working as a senior consultant with Microsoft. He has 13 years of experience in designing and developing software systems. An avid learner, he loves knowing the hows and whys of a software's design. He also likes to explore the latest technologies. Manas specializes in end-to-end delivery of cloud-based applications. More of a software purist, Manas is a proponent of designing clean, simple, and efficient architecture. Performance optimizations is one of his fortes. He holds a master's degree in information technology from IIIT-Bangalore. Outside of work, he is a sports enthusiast. Find him at `www.linkedin.com/in/manas-mayank-b966505`.

Mohit Garg is currently working as a software engineer at Microsoft. He has more than eight years of experience in Azure technologies, including .NET Core, Azure AD, Azure Data Factory, WebJobs, Functions, Azure Storage, Azure SQL, Azure Cosmos DB, and Service Fabrice. He is a Microsoft Certified Azure Developer, and he loves exploring the latest technologies. You can reach Mohit Garg at `mohitgarg2@gmail.com` or `www.linkedin.com/in/mohit-garg-36880022`

About the Technical Reviewer

Vidya Vrat Agarwal is a software architect, author, blogger, Microsoft MVP, C# Corner MVP, speaker, and mentor. He is a TOGAF certified architect and a Certified Scrum Master (CSM). He is currently working as a principal architect at T-Mobile Inc. USA. He started working on Microsoft .NET with its first beta release. Vidya is passionate about people, process, and technology and loves to contribute to the .NET community.

He lives in Redmond, WA, with his wife, Rupali, two daughters—Pearly and Arshika, and puppy Angel. He blogs at www.MyPassionFor.Net and can be reached at vidya_mct@yahoo.com or on Twitter @dotnetauthor.

Acknowledgments

I have to start by thanking my awesome wife, Samiksha Gupta. From the first day of writing this book till last day, she has supported me very well. She was as important in getting this book done as I was. Thank you so much, dear.

I would like to thank Mr. Shrenik Jhaveri, Ranjiv Sharma, and Krishna Chaitanya Telikicherla for guiding me to learn Azure technologies and Azure AD. They believed in me and constantly guided me to learn. Without their support, this book may have not been possible.

I would also like to thank my elder sister Priyanka Garg, my brother-in-law Satya Kejriwal, my younger brother Sahil Garg, and my best friends, Deep lal Sharma, Chandra Pratap Singh, Shanshu Garg, and Lucky Garg, who trusted me and encouraged me to do hard work.

I would also like to thank all the managers at Microsoft—Ashwani Sharma, Manish Sangha, Anil Emmadi, Naveen Konduri, and Pramod Walvekar—for always encouraging me to learn new technologies and to work hard. You all helped me to give a better shape to my career.

I would also like to thank my colleagues at Microsoft: Apoorv Gupta, Jebarson Jebamony, Piyush Jain, Prasad Ganganagunta, Rishabh Verma, Sachin Gupta, Kuldeep Singh, Kshitij, and Chaitanya Cheruvu. I have learned a lot from each and every one of you. Special thanks to Manas Mayank and Rahul Sawhney for motivating me to write this book.

I would also like to thank my teachers at Chitkara University for helping me to explore my potential. Thank you very much.

ACKNOWLEDGMENTS

Thanks to team at Apress Smriti Srivastava and Shrikant Vishwakarma for giving opportunity to us to write this book. Thanks to Vidya Vrat and Siddhi Chavan for doing the technical review.

—Mohit Garg

I would like to start by thanking members of my family: Bhagwan Kumar and Sanjay Poddar. Special mention of the kids: Shambhavi Poddar, Akshaj Poddar, Arush Poddar. Keep smiling.

Rahul Sawhney and Mohit Garg: if it were not for you, this book would not have been possible.

Thanks to my besties for being there: Dineshwar Singh, Vineet Anshuman, Amrita Dev, and Yogesh Sharma.

To the best people I had the opportunity to learn from: Sumeet Deshpande, Gaurav Joshi, Subhavya Sharma, Apoorv Gupta, Manojkumar Damodaran Nambisan, and Vagmi Mudumbai. Thank you.

I would like to extend my thanks to my managers and colleagues for their support: Abhishek Ghosh, Akash Sarabhai, Jebarson Jebamony, Rishabh Verma and Raviteja Jarugu.

Thanks to the faculty of my alma mater, IIT – Bengaluru (Bangalore).

Thanks to the Apress team for helping shape this book: Smriti Srivastava and Shrikant Vishwakarma. Thanks to Siddhi Chavan and Vidya Vrat for your feedback.

— Manas Mayank

Introduction

Any enterprise application worth its salt will have some kind of authentication built into it. Azure Active Directory is one of the top cloud-based identity providers on the market. It goes beyond being a traditional identity provider. Developers and architects are traditionally aware of basic authentication mechanisms, like username and password, certificate-based authentication, and so forth. This tends to influence decision-making when choosing the most appropriate authentication mechanisms for their cloud-based applications. The Internet is full of subject matter, further compounding the understanding needed for designing authentication.

This book concentrates on concepts using simple examples in its quest to bridge the distance between developers and IT infra, helping you to make the right design decisions. It is a one-stop source for getting around most relevant concepts pertaining to Azure Active Directory.

CHAPTER 1

Introduction to Azure Active Directory

The need for centralized management of users and devices over networks led to the advent of directory services. The users and devices that need to be authenticated over a network are referred to as *resources*. Directory services act as a single point that provides information about all the resources on a network.

As most of you are aware, Microsoft's implementation of on-premises directory services is called Active Directory. In this book, we will use the abbreviation AD to refer to Active Directory in general.

With the surge of solutions based on cloud-based services, there was a need for directory services that are accessible over the cloud and that are not limited to an organization's network. Microsoft's offering for identity and access management over the cloud is called Azure Active Directory (AAD). The terms Azure AD and AAD are used interchangeably for Azure Active Directory. Azure AD provides a ready-made solution to handle authentication for your cloud-based applications or mobile apps.

This book talks about how to develop applications using Azure Active Directory. In this chapter, we introduce Azure Active Directory and some key terms related to it. This will help you understand the concepts necessary for developing an application.

© Manas Mayank and Mohit Garg 2019
M. Mayank and M. Garg, *Developing Applications with Azure Active Directory*,
https://doi.org/10.1007/978-1-4842-5040-2_1

To summarize, we will define the following concepts:

- Authentication

- Authorization

- Azure Active Directory

- Tokens

- SPN

- OAuth

- OpenID Connect

- Federated identity

- Single sign-on

- Pass-through authentication

- Tenants

- Multitenancy

- Claims-based authentication

- Azure AD B2B

- Azure AD B2C

Authentication

Authentication is a process for identifying a user's identity. Authentication can be divided into two phases.

- **Identification**. During identification, the identity of the user is established using a username, email ID, mobile number, and so forth. This information is then checked to make sure that the user is valid.

- **Validation**. As part of the authentication process, the user provides credentials to identify themselves. These credentials could be in the form of a username/password, certificate, biometric information, a one-time password, and so forth.

Authentication can be divided into three categories based on the security level.

- **Single-factor authentication**. This is the traditional or simplest form of authentication, in which users enter their credentials. If the credentials are correct, then the user is authenticated to use the application.

- **Two-factor authentication**. This is a more secure way of authentication in which user credentials and another factor are needed for authentication. This could be a mobile one-time password (OTP), a security question, and so forth. User credentials with an additional factor make it nearly impossible for hackers to hack your credentials.

- **Multi-factor authentication**. This is the most secure and advanced way of authentication. In addition to your credentials, two or more additional factors are involved. None of the factors should have any relationship between them; they should be independent.

Authorization

Authorization is a process for verifying access permissions or privileges, and determining the access level that the logged-in identity has access to.

Generally, authorization is the second step after authentication. After the identity is established, a process fetches the roles/permissions/privileges related to the established identity and the required content is shown based on the user permissions. In short, authentication is the process of identifying who you are, whereas authorization is the process of determining what actions you can perform.

Authorization can be divided into two categories based on the way that permissions are given to the identity.

- **Allow authorization**. The identity has access to only those permissions that are listed; it does not have access if permission is not provided. This means that the permissions that the identity has access to are white listed, and the remaining permissions are automatically denied.

- **Deny authorization**. The identity has access to all permissions except the ones that are not given. This means that the permissions the user doesn't have access to are black listed, and the rest of the permissions are automatically allowed.

Azure Active Directory

Authentication is one of the important components in developing any enterprise application. Simple authentication for an application is rudimentary to implement. We can use a simple username and password combination stored in a database. But implementing enterprise-level authentication without using any identity provider can be very complex. You need to manage users, passwords, expiration policies, password policy management, and access management at the very least.

Things become more complicated if you use advanced concepts required for authentication, such as multi-factor authentication, one-time passwords, biometrics, and so forth. Developing these involves huge development and infrastructure costs. Moreover, maintenance and support costs are also very high. This is where established solutions like

Azure AD are most effective. Before delving deeper into Azure AD, let's discuss some key terms related to Azure Active Directory.

Tokens

An online dictionary meaning of a token is "a tangible representation of a fact." In the context of authentication, a token represents facts about the identity of a user or a resource. The set of facts is provided by directory services, which for us is Azure AD.

Tokens are used for exchanging identity information; they are signed to make them secure. They are signed using private keys and can be validated by using public keys. Tokens are valid for only a specific period to avoid misuse.

Tokens can be represented in various industry-wide formats. JSON Web Token (JWT) and Security Assertion Markup Language (SAML) are the most commonly used formats for tokens. As soon as user authentication is successful, the identity provider gives a token in response, which is valid for a specific time and signed using private keys. That token can be exchanged with other trusted systems to get access for a specific time.

A JWT token is most commonly used for integration with Azure Active Directory. As obvious by its name, a JWT token represents the user in JSON (JavaScript Object Notation) format. Here is a sample JWT token:

```
"eyJ0eXAiOiJKV1QiLCJhbGciOiJ................71846CA77+9G++/
vUjvv71q77+977+9xrMoDQo="
```

You must be wondering why this token is in plain string format and not in a JSON format. It is because the token is transformed using Base64 encoding. You need to do transformation using Base64 to see the actual JSON format.

After transformation of this token, the retrieved string is divided into three parts separated by ".". The following is a brief overview of the various fields within a token. We touch on these fields over the course of the book.

- **Headers**. Information about the type of token and the algorithm used to sign the token.

```
{
  "typ": "JWT",
  "alg": "RS256",
  "x5t": "-sxMJMLCIDWMTPvZyJ6tx-CDxwO",
  "kid": "-sxMJMLCIDWMTPvZyJ6tx-CDxwO"
}
```

  - typ: Type of token.

  - alg: Encryption Algorithm is RS256.

  - x5t: Thumbprint of public key used to sign the token.

  - kid: Like x5t. No longer part of Azure AD 2.0.

- **Payload**. Actual JWT token body.

```
{
  "aud": "https://your-resource",
  "iss": "https://sts.windows.net/72f988bf-86f1-41af-
         91ab-2d7cd011db47/",
  "iat": 1548737381,
  "nbf": 1548737381,
  "exp": 1548741279,
  "acr": "1",
  "aio":"AVQAq/8KAAAA+sqxpQOJBRhDY9/
  dmeELZJlGFvbDbfdGFB7DnFbhx5tgXdEAOxCtjF8k
  bYceM1COSkKIfBSNozYM7avIzYzoVaN/OFG22kCroWvC/
  il4QcU=",
  "amr": [
    "wia",
    "mfa"
```

```
],
"appid": "5c6035f3-e94f-4ed3-821c-40870f6cf1f3",
"appidacr": "2",
"family_name": "Scott",
"given_name": "James",
"in_corp": "true",
"ipaddr": "167.220.238.5",
"name": "Mohit Garg",
"oid": "dc5e633a-7058-474c-8f1c-435538e7d290",
"onprem_sid": "S-1-5-21-2146773085-903363285-
               719344707-2044714",
"scp": "Employees.Read.All user_impersonation",
"sub": "caF45MyAn57WqX5Omoeh9epNQ6lFKp5_xdVkjOReGIs",
"tid": "72f988bf-86f1-41af-91ab-2d7cd011db47",
"unique_name": "*****@microsoft.com",
"upn": "*****@microsoft.com",
"uti": "ktKZuwI7pkSYiAtHyiIHAA",
"ver": "1.0"
}
```

- aud. Contains the audience for which the token has been generated. It is a unique ID assigned to your application in Azure Active Directory, a.k.a. the application ID.

- iss. Identifies the issuer of the token. It's a security token service URL appended by the tenant ID. The tenant ID is a unique identifier to identify an instance of AAD.

- iat. Stands for *issued at* and means the time at which the token is issued. It's a UNIX timestamp.

- nbf. Stands for *not before* and means the token should not be accepted before this time. It is a UNIX timestamp.

- exp. Stands for *expiration time* and means the UNIX timestamp after which the token is not valid.

- acr. Stands for *authentication context class* to validate if the end user authentication meets the requirement of ISO/IES 29115 standards. A 1 means it meets and 0 means it doesn't.

- aio. Internal to Azure AD to verify if the token can be reused or not. An end user should not use this token.

- amr. A JSON array of claims contains the information about how the subject of the token will be authenticated.

- appid. Stands for *application ID*. It contains the ID of the application that has sent the request for generation of the token.

- appidacr. Indicates the mechanism used for authentication. We will discuss this in later chapters.

- family_name. Provides the last name of the user identity.

- given_name. Provides first name of the user identity.

- in_corp. A boolean claim that specifies if the request is from a corporate network or not.

- `ipaddr`. Stands for *IP address*. It provides the Internet Protocol address of the user.

- `name`. Provides the name of the user, which is used for display purposes, and it is mutable.

- `oid`. Stands for *object identifier*. It is a unique identifier for an object in Azure Active Directory. It is in the form of GUID. It can be used as a unique key in a database to identify the user.

  `onprem_sid`. If on-premise authentication is used, then the claim has this identifier. It is used for legacy applications. SID is outside the scope of this book. For more information, please refer to `https://docs.microsoft.com/en-us/windows/desktop/SecAuthZ/sid-components`.

- `scp`. Stands for *scopes* and means a set of scopes exposed by the application for which the request user or client has access to. Scopes are returned in a space separated string.

- `sub`. Stands for *subject*. It's a unique string for the combination of a user and an application. It is immutable and can be used as a unique key in a database for authorization purposes. It is different from an object identifier, which is unique for each user.

- `tid`. Stands for *tenant ID*. This is discussed later in this chapter.

- `unique_name`. Present only in Azure AD v1. A claim name is both unique and not unique. It is a human-readable value that identifies the subject; it should be used only for display purposes.

- upn. Stands for *user principal name*. This is
  discussed later in this chapter.

- uti. An internal claim used by Azure AD to
  revalidate a token. An end user should not use this
  token.

- ver. Stands for *version*. Indicates the version of the
  access token. It can be either 1.0 or 2.0.

- **Signature**. Signed token content for validating the
  authenticity using a public key. A token issued by Azure
  AD is signed with an asymmetric encryption algorithm,
  as shown in Figure 1-1.

```
Zl♦CW`] ♦Pl♦l(wE♦l♦S♦>ˠ♦f9♦♦@♦♦p♦♦8l♦♦^Hⅈlm♦♦Q%O♦♦\♦♦."♦e?z♦Dl\♦♦M{:♦l♦♦6♦w
♦l/♦U♦♦@♦♦\♦x♦♦♦6♦_
y♦♦♦♦♦♦♦@ⅈS♦♦♦l♦l7>♦♦♦|e3♦♦♦x♦rˇVⅈ♦@E♦♦♦♦b♦oc.♦♦]♦Jꜱ♦b♦♦♦♦*!♦♦P♦/7♦♦♦♦ⅈl)♦@ⅈ♦1ⅈ♦ⅉF,♦♦*H♦bꜱ(Eg♦*♦♦♦♦♦ⅈe♦b.qⅈ♦l'♦9rⅈ♦♦P♦(ⅈGX♦%♦|儱♦l♦H♦j♦♦Y(
```

Figure 1-1. *Encrypted token*

Note   A token is not in human-readable format, because it is a raw
material required for validation of the token.

SPN

SPN stands for *service principal name*. To access any resource that is
secured by Azure Active Directory, you need a security principal. A
security principal defines the permissions and access policies, which
in turn help to enable Azure AD core features like authentication and
authorization. The security principal defined for an application is known
as a *service principal*. The SPN is required to access resources secured by
Azure AD. Access resources secured by Azure AD using an application
service principal are explained later in this book.

OAuth

OAuth stands for *open authorization.* It's an open standard for token-based authentication and authorization. It allows you to authorize third-party applications by sharing a token containing logged-in user information instead of the actual username and password. It was first released in December 2007 as OAuth Core 1.0.

The second version of the OAuth standard (OAuth 2.0) was released five years later. It is not backward compatible with OAuth 1.0. OAuth 2.0 has new authorization flows for web applications, mobile applications, desktop applications, and smart devices.

Please refer to `https://oauth.net/2/` to read more about OAuth and OAuth 2.0.

OpenID Connect

OpenID Connect, also known as OIDC, is built on top of the OAuth 2.0 protocol. It defines standards for authentication based on JSON and HTTP protocols. It helps verify the identity of the logged-in user compared to the authorization it has over resources. It can provide basic information about the logged-in user using the REST API.

OIDC allows different types of clients, including web clients, mobile clients, and JavaScript clients to perform authentication and to request and receive information about logged-in users and authenticated sessions.

Please refer to `https://openid.net/connect/` to learn more about OpenID Connect.

Federated Identity

Consider a scenario where a single user might need to authenticate in multiple organizations. Each of these organizations has different identity providers. A user's credentials are stored in its parent identity management system. Other identity providers can trust the parent identity management system and allow the user to be validated in multiple organizations. A federation refers to the protocols used to achieve this scenario. The user identity provided by such a system is called a *federated identity*.

Single Sign-On

Single sign-on, or SSO, allows users to use one set of credentials to log in to multiple applications. After authenticating, users do not need to reauthenticate for other applications. This streamlines user experiences and gives administrators better control over user identities. Protocols like OAuth and OpenID Connect can work on applications in various platforms to provide a seamless single sign-on experience.

Pass-Through Authentication

Pass-through authentication allows users to authenticate against an on-prem Active Directory using AAD. Azure AD doesn't save the username and password. Whenever a user tries to sign in, Azure AD forwards the request to an on-prem Active Directory so that the user can be authenticated.

Tenant

In layman's terms, *tenant* means a person who possesses a property or land from a landlord. Similarly, in the world of identity management, a tenant is a representation of an organization in the identity management system. Multiple organizations can register and create their own tenant in Azure Active Directory. A tenant can have multiple users from the same organization.

Multitenancy

Multitenancy refers to a single application consumed by users from different organizations. One tenant develops the application and can invite other tenants to use the same application. Multitenancy is a huge topic that is discussed in a chapter later in this book.

Claims-Based Authentication

Claims are a set of information that describes a given resource's identity. It's a set of key/value pairs related to the logged-in identity (user or app), for example, the user's principal name, email address, groups, first name, last name, and so forth.

In the context of Azure Active Directory, applications get claims after successful authentication using OAuth 2.0 and OpenID Connect. In web applications, claims are stored in a cookie in a secured manner to perform claims-based authentication for further requests.

Microsoft released claims-based authentication with .NET Framework 3.0. The basic authentication flow shown in Figure 1-2 is for claims-based authentication using Azure Active Directory.

1. The user makes a request to the web application.

2. The user is redirected to the Azure AD login page.

3. After successful authentication, Azure AD redirects the user with a token that has user-related claims.

4. The claims are stored in cookie in a secure fashion.

5. The web application does the authentication using claims and returns the response if the claims are valid.

13

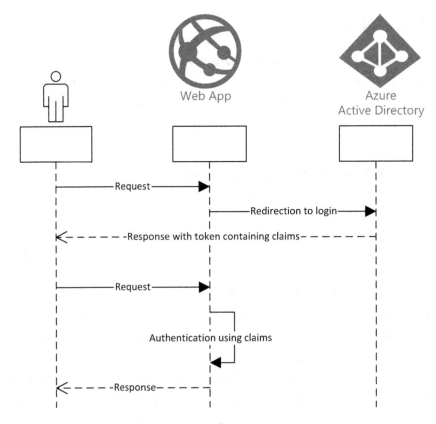

Figure 1-2. *Basic authentication flow*

Azure AD B2B

B2B refers to business to business. If you need to securely share your company's applications and services with other companies or guest users, you can use Azure AD B2B. You have full control over your organization's data. You can invite users from another organization, also using Azure AD. Organizations not using Azure Active Directory can be added as a guest user in the tenant. Partner users use their own identity management solution. There is no need for any additional overhead from your organization to maintain partner users.

Invited users are able to use their own credentials to log in to your application and services. You can customize your solution for inviting users by using Azure AD B2B invite APIs.

The following are the advantages of using Azure AD B2B collaboration.

- You can invite any user with a valid email address. It is not mandatory to be an Azure AD user.

- There is no need to manage external user accounts or their identity providers.

- After the invitation, there is no need to sync accounts or manage policies.

- External AD users are able to use the same credentials. There is no need to manage different credentials for different applications.

- If an invited user doesn't have any associated AD or live account, an account will be created for them after accepting the invitation.

Developing applications using the Azure Active Directory business-to-business collaboration is explained later.

Azure AD B2C

B2C stands for business-to-customer collaboration. If you need to create a customer-facing application, you should use Azure AD B2C. Azure B2C is based on similar components as AAD, but its core purpose is to provide identity management for an organization's customers. Users of Azure AD B2C are able to log in with an existing identity (from external providers like Facebook, Twitter, Google, Outlook, LinkedIn, etc.). There is no need for a separate Azure AD user account; the same identity (username and password) can be used to log in.

Summary

Various Azure services can integrate with Azure AD and use it as an identity provider. Azure AD is used as an identity provider by Microsoft SaaS services like Office 365. It can also be integrated with third-party SaaS solutions like Salesforce. In addition to SaaS solutions, Azure AD can be used with Azure VMs and various Azure PaaS services. Furthermore, Azure AD can be synchronized with on-premises Active Directory.

This chapter focused on introducing readers to the fundamentals of authentication and Azure AD in a simple language. We started by introducing the meaning of authentication and authorization to understand the purpose of Azure Active Directory and related technologies, such as Azure AD B2B and Azure AD B2C. We also touched on various standards, such OAuth, OpenID, and OpenID Connect. Before getting deeper into any technology, you should understand its various standards and protocols.

We shall continue our journey by learning more about OAuth standards in the next chapter.

CHAPTER 2

OAuth Flows and OpenID Connect

In Chapter 1, we defined key terms related to Azure Active Directory. Before getting into the practical details of any technology, you must understand the standards that the technology is based upon. In this chapter, we will cover the following topics.

- OAuth 2.0

- OAuth 2.0 Grant Types

  - Authorization code

  - Implicit

  - Resource owner password credentials

  - Client credentials

- OpenID Connect

  - OpenID Connect metadata documents

  - Authentication flows using OpenID Connect

- Tokens

  - Validating tokens

To integrate applications with Azure AD, you must first understand the OAuth and OpenID Connect standards.

© Manas Mayank and Mohit Garg 2019
M. Mayank and M. Garg, *Developing Applications with Azure Active Directory*,
https://doi.org/10.1007/978-1-4842-5040-2_2

OAuth 2.0

OAuth 2.0 standards are not backward compatible with OAuth 1.0. The differences between the two are beyond the scope of this book. We will concentrate on the latest OAuth 2.0 standards.

To understand the need for OAuth, let's consider a real-world scenario. Assume that you work for an organization that provides authorized access to employees over secured areas. Employees swipe smart cards provided by the organization's security team to gain access to secured physical spaces. When a visitor comes to see an employee, the visitor provides her information, and the employee provides her credentials (along with the employee's smart card) to the representative of the security team. Security personnel then issue a temporary visiting identity card to the visitor, allowing her to enter the physical premises for a limited period. This real-world scenario is roughly represented by the sequence diagram shown in Figure 2-1.

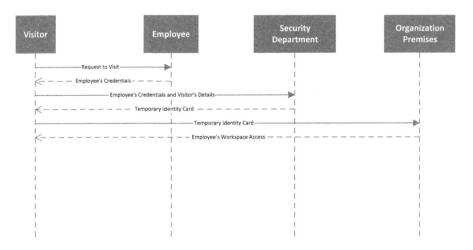

Figure 2-1. *Visitor access scenario*

If a third party (the client) needs to access a user's (the resource owner) resources from the server hosting the user's resources (a resource server), they will get a separate set of credentials (a token) from another server (an authorization server) that is trusted by the resource server.

OAuth was designed to allow access to user resources by using another set of credentials of the user's credentials. Older systems needed users to provide their credentials (for example, username and password), explicitly to the third party trying to access the user's resources. The OAuth protocol evolved to address these concerns and has the following advantages over earlier standards.

- Earlier standards of storing username/password with a third party gave the third party unlimited access to the user's resources.

- Revoking access equated to changing the password.

- Risk from security perspective as password would be stored at multiple places

The sequence diagram shown in Figure 2-2 depicts the OAuth flow.

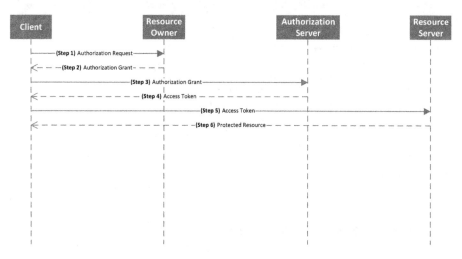

Figure 2-2. OAuth flow

As depicted in Figure 2-2, the following are the actors or roles in OAuth flow.

- **Client**. An application trying to access a user's resources on behalf of the user. It does so by using tokens. We discuss tokens in a subsequent section.

- **Resource owner**. The user or application that is the owner of a resource. The resource is stored on the resource server.

- **Authorization server**. After authenticating the resource owner, provides the token to the client for accessing the resource.

- **Resource server**. The server that hosts a resource owned by the resource owner.

If we map our real-world visitor scenario, the sequence diagram could be merged, as shown in Figure 2-3.

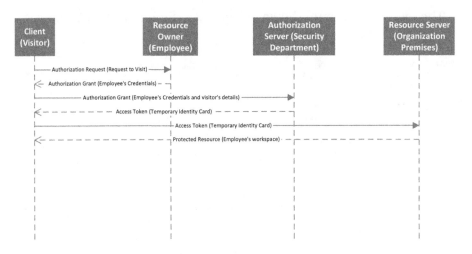

Figure 2-3. *Merged sequence diagram*

We will use the basic OAuth flow sequence diagram (see Figure 2-2) as a reference for explaining each of the steps.

OAuth 2.0 Grant Types

The client accesses the resource owner's resources by using an access token. For the client to get this access token, it must receive authorization from the resource owner. These credentials, which represent the resource owner's authorization, are called an *authorization grant*. An authorization grant defines how an application gets an access token. It is used in steps 2 and 3 of the basic OAuth flow, as highlighted in Figure 2-4.

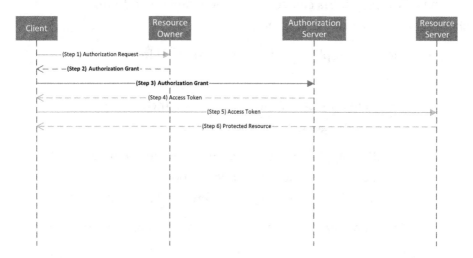

Figure 2-4. Basic OAuth flow

OAuth specification defines four different authorization grant types or four different ways of getting access tokens. These types define the process used to get an access token.

- Authorization code

- Implicit

- Resource owner password credentials

- Client credentials

We discuss each of these grant types in this chapter. This chapter also introduces OAuth 2.0 standards. Azure AD–specific details are covered in subsequent chapters.

Authorization Code Grant

An authorization code grant is one of the most common grant flows used. It deals with scenarios where the client application is deployed on a web server and the actual code is not exposed publicly.

The following criteria can be used as general preconditions for choosing an authorization code grant.

- The client application is a web app served from a web server.

- The client application can interact with the resource owner agent, generally a web browser.

- The client application can securely save the client ID and client secret, without publicly exposing them. We talk about client IDs and client secrets in later sections.

- The client application can react to the resource owner's actions.

- The client application is capable of receiving requests from the authorization server, generally via redirection.

The diagram shown in Figure 2-5 details the process of an authorization code flow. The following are the actors in the authorization code flow (the corresponding actors from the previous section are in parentheses).

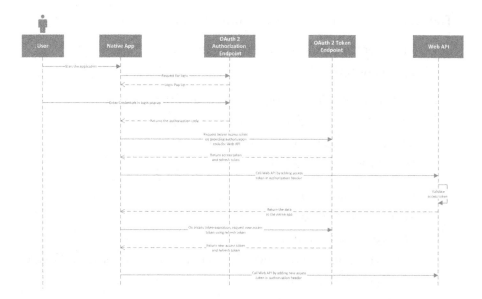

Figure 2-5. *Process for authorization code flow*

- **User (resource owner).** The owner of the resource. The user interacts with the client application via a user agent (browser).

- **Client application (client).** This is a web application trying to access a secured resource. The client application can also be a native app.

- **OAuth 2 Authorization endpoint/Token endpoint (authorization server).** Different authorization server endpoints used to get different kinds of tokens.

- **Web API (resource server).** API providing the resource owned by the resource owner.

The following are the steps for an authorization code grant.

1. The user tries to access and log in through the client application URL.

2. The client application redirects the unauthenticated user to the authorization endpoint of the authorization server. The client constructs a request URI in the following format.

```
https://aad-tenant/authorize?
response_type=code
  &client_id=client123
  &redirect_uri=https%3A%2F%2Fclient-application%2Fcallback
  &scope=read+write
  &state=abc
```

Table 2-1 describes the significance of each of the parameters.

Table 2-1. *Parameter Descriptions*

Sr. No.	Parameter	Required/ Optional	Description
1.	response_type	Required	Should be set to "code" for code grant flow.
2.	client_id	Required	The client application must be registered with the authorization server to access secured resources. The client_id is a unique ID, by which the authorization server uniquely identifies the client application, which is provided by the authorization server. We discuss the process of registration on Azure AD in Chapter 3.

(continued)

Table 2-1. (*continued*)

Sr. No.	Parameter	Required/ Optional	Description
3.	redirect_uri	Optional	After authenticating the resource owner, the authorization server redirects the browser to this URI.
4.	Scope	Optional	Scope is a list of case-sensitive strings delimited by space. It defines the permissions requested by the client. Possible values for the scope are predefined on the authorization server.
5.	State	Recommended	A random string included by the client in the request. The authorization server includes this string when redirecting a user agent to the client application. The client validates if the string is the same as the request. It is used to avoid cross-site request forgery (CSRF).

3. The authorization server redirects the user to log in and prompts the user to authenticate.

4. The user enters his credentials for authentication.

5. Assuming that user authentication is successful, the authorization server redirects the user agent to the URI, which is specified in the redirect_uri parameter in step 3. The response format is as follows.

```
https:// client-application/callback?
code=xyz123
&state=abc
```

Table 2-2 describes the significance of each of the parameters.

Table 2-2. *Parameter Descriptions*

S.No.	Parameter	Required/ Optional	Description
1.	code	Required	This is the authorization code generated by the authorization server; it can be used only once. The code should have a limited lifetime; the maximum recommended lifetime is 10 minutes. It is generated for the combination of the client_id and redirect_uri parameters of the request (see step 2).
2.	state	Required	The same value that was sent in the request parameter (see step 2).

6. After receiving the authorization code in the previous step, the client application requests an access token from the token endpoint of the authorization server by using a post request and exchanging the authorization code. The format of the request is as follows.

    ```
    https://aad-tenant/token
    ```

    The parameters of the post request are shown in Table 2-3.

Table 2-3. *Parameter Descriptions*

S.No.	Parameter	Required/ Optional	Description
1.	grant_type	Required	Should be set to authorization_code.
2.	code	Required	The authorization code, as received in the authorization response in step 5.
3.	redirect_uri	Required	Same as the authorization code request in step 2. Should be included if it was present in the original authorization code request.
4.	client_id	Required	Unique ID, by which the authorization server uniquely identifies the client application. The same as the authorization request in step 2.
5.	client_secret	Required	The client application is registered with the authorization server. As part of the completion of the registration process, the authorization server generates client_id and client_secret for the client application. While client_id uniquely identifies the application and can be publicly visible, client_secret is confidential. Consider client_id and client_secret equivalent to a username and password, respectively.

7. If the authorization token request is successful, the authorization server sends the response back to the client application. The response is in the following format.

```
{
        "access_token": "abc123",
        "token_type": "bearer",
        "expires_in": 3600,
        "refresh_token": "xyz890",
        "scope": "read write"
}
```

Table 2-4 shows the significance of each of the parameters.

Table 2-4. *Parameter Descriptions*

S.No.	Parameter	Required/ Optional	Description
1.	access_token	Required	The access token returned by the authorization server. We discuss token IDs in later sections.
2.	token_type	Required	The only value supported by Azure AD is "bearer". It signifies the type of token understood by the client. Further information is beyond the scope of this book.
3.	expires_in	Recommended	The lifetime (in seconds) that a token is valid. The token expires after this period.
4.	refresh_token	Optional	After the token expires, a refresh token could be utilized to get a new access token. They are long-lasting and bound to the client application to which they were issued.
5.	scope	Optional	The same as the scope specified by the client in the authorization code request in step 2.

8. After getting the access code, the client uses the access token to access the Web API. We briefly touched on tokens in Chapter 1. Headers of all requests to the API should include the Authorization header.

    `"Authorization: Bearer eyJ0..."`

    Depending on the validating token, the API could either allow access to the resource or throw an error.

9. If the access token has expired or is invalid, the client application can request another access token by sending a refresh token. The client does so by sending a post request to the token endpoint of the authorization server. The request's parameters are described in Table 2-5.

Table 2-5. *Parameter Descriptions*

S.No.	Parameter	Required/ Optional	Description
1.	grant_type	Required	Should be set to refresh_token.
2.	refresh_ token	Required	The refresh token sent by the authorization server to the client application. This is the same as refresh_token, which is received while requesting the access token in step 7.
3.	scope	Optional	Considered the same as the original request, if not included. You can't add a value that was not in the original request for the access token.

10. In the event of a successful request, the
authorization server returns the response in the
same format as when the request for the access
token was made (the same as step 7.)

Implicit Grant

This flow is typically used by applications implemented using scripting
languages like JavaScript. The secured resource is directly accessed using
the scripting language. An implicit grant is a variant of an authorization
code grant flow. But instead of having separate requests for getting the
authorization code and the access token, the access token is received after
authorizing with the "authorize" endpoint. There is no separate client_id
and client_secret authentication. Since the access token is exposed to the
resource owner and the other application on the client device, an implicit
grant is considered less secure. Since it is less secure, an implicit grant flow
does not use a refresh token.

The following criteria are the general rules for choosing an implicit
grant.

- The client application accesses resources by using
  scripting languages like JavaScript. Single-page
  applications are recommended to use this flow.

- Client applications are a hybrid of post-back-based web
  applications. They also use AJAX calls to refresh pages
  from different resource APIs.

- The client application can react to the resource owner's
  actions.

- The client application is capable of receiving requests
  from the authorization server, generally via redirection.

The diagram shown in Figure 2-6 details the process flow for an implicit grant. The following are the actors for the implicit grant flow (the mapping of the actors defined in Figure 2-3 are in parentheses).

- **User (resource owner)**. The owner of the resource. The user interacts with the client application via a user agent (browser).

- **Client application (client)**. A web application trying to access a secured resource. The client application is JavaScript-based (or SPA).

- **OAuth 2 Authorization endpoint (authorization server)**. The endpoint of the authorization server used to get access tokens.

- **Web API (resource server)**. API providing the resource owned by the resource owner.

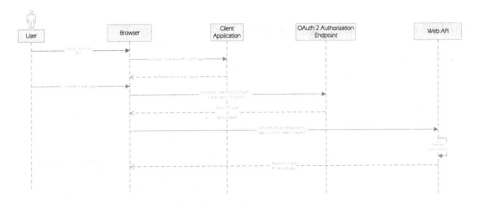

Figure 2-6. *Process flow for implicit grant*

The following are the steps for an implicit grant.

1. The user tries to access and log in through the client application URL.

2. The client application redirects the unauthenticated user to the authorization endpoint of the authorization server. The client constructs a request URI in the following format.

```
https://aad-tenant/authorize?
response_type=token
  &client_id=client123
  &redirect_uri=https%3A%2F%2Fclient-application%2Fcallback
  &scope=read+write
  &state=abc
```

Table 2-6 describes the significance of each of the parameters.

Table 2-6. *Parameter Descriptions*

S.No.	Parameter	Required/ Optional	Description
1.	response_type	Required	Should be set to "token" for an implicit grant flow vs. "code" for a code grant flow.
2.	client_id	Required	The client application must be registered with the authorization server to access secured resources. The client_id is a unique ID by which the authorization server uniquely identifies the client application. It is provided by the authorization server. We discuss the process of registration on Azure AD in Chapter 3.

(continued)

Table 2-6. (*continued*)

S.No.	Parameter	Required/ Optional	Description
3.	redirect_uri	Optional	After authenticating the resource owner, the authorization server redirects the browser to this URI.
4.	scope	Optional	Scope is a list of case-sensitive strings delimited by space. It defines the permissions being requested by the client. Possible values for the scope are predefined on the authorization server.
5.	state	Recommended	This is a random string included by the client in the request. The authorization server includes this string when redirecting a user agent to the client application. The client validates the string the same as the request. This is used to avoid cross-site request forgery.

3. The authorization server redirects the user to log in and prompts the user to authenticate.

4. The user enters his credentials for authentication.

5. Assuming that user authentication is successful, the authorization server redirects the user agent to the URI specified in the redirect_uri, as follows.

```
https:// client-application/callback#
access_token =xyz123
& token_type =bearer
```

```
&expires_in=3600
&scope= read+write
&state=abc
```

Note that there is no refresh token returned.

Table 2-7 describes the significance of each of the parameters.

Table 2-7. *Parameter Description*

S.No.	Parameter	Required/ Optional	Description
1.	access_token	Required	The implicit grant flow returns the access token instead of the authorization code. Also, note that the token is returned as a query fragment (vs. a query parameter).
2.	token_type	Required	The only value supported by Azure AD is "bearer". It signifies the type of token understood by the client. Further information is beyond the scope of this book.
3.	expires_in	Recommended	The lifetime (in seconds) that a token is valid. The token expires after this period.
4.	scope	Optional	Considered the same as the original request, if not included. We can't add a value that was not in the original request for the access token.
5.	state	Required	The same value that was sent in the request parameter (see step 2).

6.   After getting the access token, the client uses the access token to access the Web API.

Resource Owner Password Credentials Grant

The *resource owner password credentials grant,* or simply *password grant,* is one of the simplest grant flows. This grant requires the resource owner to provide a username and password to the client application. Since the resource owner's credentials are exposed to the client application, the resource owner should trust the client application. A password grant is generally used for internal client applications; it should not be used with third-party applications. The following are use cases for which a password grant is applicable.

- The resource owner has a trust relationship with the client application.

- The services and applications trying to access a resource API belong to the same resource API provider.

- Migrate older username and password–based applications to use OAuth.

- Secure client application devices using a username and password by storing the access token (with a specific expiration time) and using an access token to access the resource API, instead of prompting for a username and password on each login.

The diagram shown in Figure 2-7 details the process flow for a password grant. The following are the actors for the password grant flow (the mapping to the actors defined in Figure 2-3 is in parentheses).

- **User (resource owner).** The owner of the resource. The user interacts with the client application via a user agent (browser).

- **Client application (client).** This is a web application trying to access a secured resource.

- **OAuth 2 Authorization endpoint (authorization server).** The endpoint of the authorization server used to get the access token.

- **Web API (resource server).** API providing the resource owned by the resource owner.

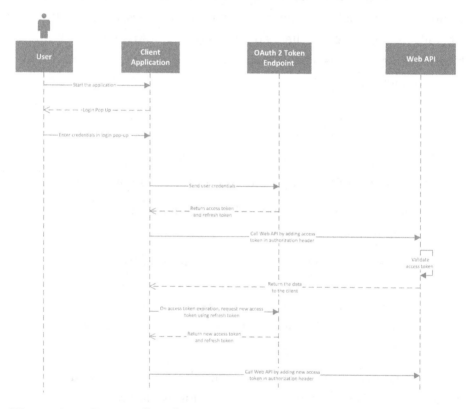

Figure 2-7. *Process flow for password grant*

The following are the steps for a password grant.

1. The user tries to access and log in through the client application URL.

2. The client application displays a form to enter the username and password.

3. The user enters her username and password and tries to log in.

4. The client application sends a post request to the Web API with the parameters shown in Table 2-8.

Table 2-8. *Parameter Descriptions*

S.No.	Parameter	Required/ Optional	Description
1.	grant_type	Required	Should be set to "password".
2.	username	Required	The username for the resource name.
3.	password	Required	The password for the resource name.
4.	scope	Optional	Scope is a list of case-sensitive strings delimited by space. It defines the permissions being requested by the client. Possible values for scope are predefined on the authorization server.

5. If the authorization token request is successful, the authorization server sends the response back to the client application. The response is in the following format.

```
{
        "access_token": "abc123",
        "token_type": "bearer",
        "expires_in": 3600,
        "refresh_token": "xyz890",
        "scope": "read write"
}
```

Table 2-9 describes the significance of each of the parameters.

Table 2-9. *Parameter Descriptions*

S.No.	Parameter	Required/ Optional	Description
1.	access_ token	Required	The access token returned by the authorization server.
2.	token_type	Required	Signifies the type of token understood by the client. Further information is beyond the scope of this book.
3.	expires_in	Recommended	The lifetime (in seconds) that a token is valid. The token expires after this period.
4.	refresh_ token	Optional	After the token expires, a refresh token could be utilized to get a new access token. They are long-lasting and bound to the client application to which they were issued.
5.	scope	Optional	The same as the scope specified by the client in post request in step 4.

6. After getting the access token, the client uses the access token to access the Web API.

Client Credentials

At times, the client application needs to access a resource as itself. In such a scenario, the client application will not need any user-specific credentials. For example, the application might want to display certain information that is common for all users but specific to the client application itself.

The diagram shown in Figure 2-8 details the process flow for a password grant. The following are the actors for the password grant flow (the mapping to the actors defined in Figure 2-2 is in parentheses).

- **Client application (client)**. A web application trying to access a secured resource.

- **OAuth 2 Authorization endpoint (authorization server)**. The endpoint of the authorization server used to get the access token.

- **Web API (resource server)**. API providing the resource owned by the resource owner.

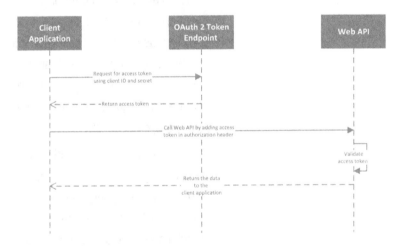

Figure 2-8. *Process flow for password grant*

The following are the steps for a client credentials grant.

1. Client application sends a post request to the token endpoint of the Web API to get an access token. The parameters of the post request are described in Table 2-10.

Table 2-10. *Parameter Descriptions*

S.No.	Parameter	Required/ Optional	Description
1.	grant_type	Required	Should be set to client_credentials.
2.	client_id	Required	A unique ID by which the authorization server uniquely identifies the client application.
3.	client_secret	Required	The client application is registered with the authorization server. As part of registration process completion, the authorization server generates client_id and client_secret for the client application. While the client_id uniquely identifies the application and can be publicly visible, client_secret is confidential. Consider client_id and client_secret equivalent to username and password, respectively.
4.	scope	Optional	Scope is a list of case-sensitive strings delimited by space. It defines the permissions being requested by the client. Possible values for the scope are predefined on the authorization server.

2. If the request is successful, the authorization server
sends the response back to the client application.
The response is in the following format.

```
{
        "access_token": "abc123",
        "token_type": "bearer",
        "expires_in": 3600,
        "scope": "read write"
}
```

Table 2-11 indicates the significance of each of the
parameters.

Table 2-11. *Parameter Descriptions*

S.No.	Parameter	Required/ Optional	Description
1.	access_ token	Required	The access token returned by the authorization server.
2.	token_type	Required	The only value supported by Azure AD is "bearer". It signifies the type of token understood by the client. Further information is beyond the scope of this book.
3.	expires_in	Recommended	The lifetime (in seconds) that a token is valid. The token expires after this period.
4.	scope	Optional	The same as the scope specified by the client in post request in step 1.

3. After getting the access token, the client uses it to
access the Web API.

41

OpenID Connect

OpenID Connect, also known as OIDC, is a simple identity layer on top of the OAuth 2.0 protocol. It helps verify the identity of the logged in user based on the authentication performed by an authorization server. It can also get basic information about the logged-in user by using the REST API.

OIDC allows different types of clients—including web clients, mobile clients, and JavaScript clients—to perform authentication and to request and receive information about logged-in users and authenticated sessions.

OpenID Connect Metadata Document

OpenID Connect offers a metadata document that provides all the necessary information required for logging in. This document can be obtained for any tenant from the following URL in Azure AD: https://login.microsoftonline.com/{tenant}/.well-known/openid-configuration.

The following is a sample metadata document.

```
{
"authorization_endpoint": "https://login.microsoftonline.com/
{tenantId}/oauth2/authorize",
"token_endpoint": "https://login.microsoftonline.com/
{tenantId}/oauth2/token",
  "token_endpoint_auth_methods_supported": [
    "client_secret_post",
    "private_key_jwt",
    "client_secret_basic"
  ],

. . . . . . . . . . . . . . . . . . .

}
```

Authentication Flow Using OpenID Connect

A basic authentication flow using OpenID Connect involves a web application in which the user logs in and a Web API that is accessed by using an access token.

The sequence diagram shown in Figure 2-9 explains the basic authentication flow in detail.

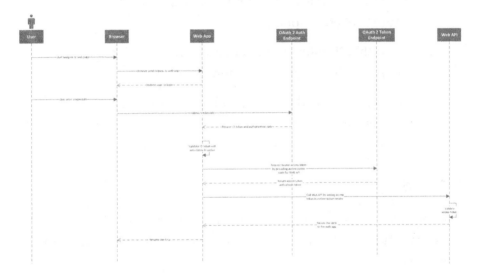

Figure 2-9. *Basic authentication flow*

The following are the steps involved.

1. The user navigates to the URL in the browser.

2. The browser sends a request to the web page.

3. The user is redirected to a login page.

4. The user enters her credentials and submits them in the browser.

5. The browser submits the credentials to the OAuth 2 Authorization endpoint.

43

6. On successful verification of the credentials, the OAuth 2 endpoint issues an ID token and an authorization code to the web application.

7. The web app validates the ID token and sets the claims in a cookie.

8. The web app requests a bearer access token for the Web API by using an authorization code to the OAuth 2 token endpoint.

9. The Web API validates the access token by getting public keys from the OAuth endpoint.

10. On successful validation, the API returns the data to the user via the web app.

Tokens

We introduced you to JWT tokens in Chapter 1. Azure Active Directory makes use of JWT tokens in various authentication flows. Basically, there are three types of tokens.

- **ID token**. During authentication with OpenID Connect, ID tokens are sent to client applications to authenticate the user. For a web application, ID tokens are stored in a cookie to authenticate further client requests from the same session.

  ID tokens validate the user and get additional information (claims) about the authenticated user. Information inside can be used to show the display name, get the unique identifier for further authorizations, and so forth. The ID token for JSON is similar to what we explained in Chapter 1.

- **Access token.** Access tokens access Web APIs secured by Azure Active Directory. When authenticating with an OpenID Connect authentication flow, the access token is returned with an ID token. The ID token is stored in a cookie, whereas an access token can instantly access a Web API, or it can be stored in a server-side cache to call the Web API for further requests from the same user.

  Access tokens authenticate the Web API. After successful validation, the application gets information about the user and the client from which the request is coming. Based on the request can be served.

  The access token is valid for one hour. After one hour, if the user still wants to access the Web API, he needs log in again, or a refresh token can be stored in the cache to generate the access token again.

- **Refresh token**. An access token is valid for one hour, which can't be extended. To avoid re-logging in every hour, refresh tokens are maintained. Refresh tokens are also issued by Azure Active Directory along with ID tokens and access tokens.

  The validity of a refresh token is a sliding 5 days to a maximum of 90 days. As its name suggests, the purpose of a refresh token is to refresh an access token. A refresh token should not be used for any other purpose.

Validating Tokens

An ID token and an access token should be validated, but there is no need to validate a refresh token.

The first step in validating an access or ID token is to validate the signature. Signature validation verifies that there was no tampering during transit.

Azure AD libraries validate the signature by using public keys available from the tenant URL and the OpenID Connect metadata document, which is at `https://login.microsoftonline.com/common/.well-known/openid-configuration`. This is a JSON document that has the information required for signature validation.

Other things that should be validated are the expiry, audience, and resources for which the access token is generated. By using claims from the access token and the ID token, further authorization can be performed.

Summary

In this chapter, we covered the various standards used by Azure Active Directory. We started by discussing OAuth 2.0 grant flows to OpenID Connect, and then described different types of tokens. Starting in Chapter 3, we discuss the implementation of these standards in Azure AD, and we delve into code.

CHAPTER 3

User-Based Authentication for Web Apps

In Chapter 2, we introduced OpenID Connect, OAuth 2, and basic authentication flows supported by OAuth 2. In this chapter, we will use those authentication flows to develop user-based authentication for a web application using Azure Active Directory. The following authentication scenarios are covered in this chapter.

- Single-page application

- Web app/Web API

- Web app/Azure Function HTTP endpoint

- Web app/Web API 1/Web API 2

We also discuss the need for multi-factor authentication and how to enable it for users in Azure Active Directory.

© Manas Mayank and Mohit Garg 2019
M. Mayank and M. Garg, *Developing Applications with Azure Active Directory*,
https://doi.org/10.1007/978-1-4842-5040-2_3

Single-Page Application

Single-page applications (SPAs) are web apps that load a single HTML page and dynamically update that page as the user interacts with the app. SPAs use AJAX and HTML5 to create fluid and responsive web apps, without constant page reloads. However, this means much of the work happens on the client side in JavaScript. It has multiple web pages, which are loaded dynamically through JavaScript and APIs. Gmail, Facebook, GitHub, and so forth, are the best examples of single-page applications. The biggest advantage of single-page applications is that no reloading of pages means no wait time.

Single-page applications heavily rely on client-side JavaScript. SPAs are backed by the Web API, where actual business logic and database transactions are handled. Implementing authentication for a JavaScript-based, client-side library is bit tricky, but Azure Active Directory Authentication Library for JavaScript (ADAL JS) makes it very simple. ADAL JS is an open source library that can be downloaded from https:// github.com/AzureAD/azure-activedirectory-library-for-js.

ADAL JS makes use of implicit grant flows to implement authentication for single-page applications. The JavaScript client communicates with Azure Active Directory to authenticate the user and get an ID token, which authenticates the Web API. The token is cached in local storage and used for subsequent requests. Figure 3-1 is a diagram of the sequence of events that happen when authenticating single-page applications using Azure Active Directory.

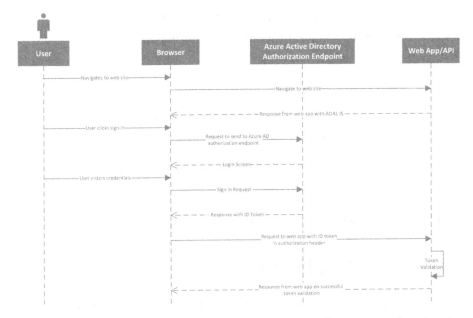

Figure 3-1. *Sequence diagram for single-page application authentication*

The following sequence of events are performed during authentication.

1. The user navigates to the web application.

2. The web application returns the web page with the JavaScript-based ADAL JS.

3. The user clicks a sign-in button or performs a secure operation.

4. The request is sent to an Azure AD authorization endpoint.

5. The user is redirected to the login page.

6. The user enters credentials and submits the sign-in request to the Azure Active Directory authorization endpoint.

7. On successful validation of the credentials, the Azure AD authorization endpoint returns the response with an ID token.

8. The ID token is stored in local storage.

9. The request with an ID token in the authorization header is sent to the API inside the same web app.

10. The API, which is secured by Azure Active Directory authentication, validates the token.

11. On successful validation, a response is returned.

Running the Application

To develop a single-page application using Azure Active Directory authentication, you need the following software and completed prerequisites.

- Visual Studio 2017 (If you don't have a license, you can use the Community edition.)

- .NET Core 2.1 SDK

- an Azure subscription and an Azure AD tenant

- a user account in your Azure AD tenant

The first step is to register the application with Azure AD. The following is a step-by-step demonstration of registering your application with Azure AD.

1. Go to `https://portal.azure.com`.

2. Go to Azure Active Directory in the left navigation pane.

3. Click App Registrations.

4. Click New Registration.

5. Enter the name of your application, which can be
    changed later.

6. Enter **http://localhost:53342** as the redirect URL,
    and choose Web in the drop-down menu.

7. Click Register.

8. Copy the application ID. It is a client ID for your
    application and required for logging in.

9. Grant permissions to your application in API
    Permissions and click the Grant Admin Consent
    button. Click Yes to confirm.

10. To find the tenant ID, go to App Registrations.
    Click Endpoints. Fetch the tenant ID
    from any URL. A sample format is at
    https://login.microsoftonline.com/
    {tenantId}/federationmetadata/2007-06/
    federationmetadata.xml. The tenant ID is always a
    valid GUID.

11. By default, implicit grant flow is disabled in Azure
    apps. To enable implicit grant flow, go to the app
    and click Manifest. Open the inline Manifest editor.
    Search for "oauth2AllowImplicitFlow" and change
    the value from false to true. Click Save.

The configurations are ready. The next step is to create a single-page
application and enable Azure Active Directory authentication for it.

Creating a Single-Page Application

To create a single-page application, follow these steps.

1. Create a Web API MVC application using .NET Core 2.0.

2. Install the Microsoft.IdentityModel.Clients. ActiveDirectory package from NuGet (www.nuget. org).

3. Add the AzureAdOptions class to read the config, as shown in the following format.

```
public class AzureAdOptions
    {
public string ClientId { get; set; }
public string ClientSecret { get; set; }
public string Instance { get; set; }
public string Domain { get; set; }
public string TenantId { get; set; }
    }
```

- Add the configuration in appsettings.json in the following format. Fill in the configuration values as per the registration done in the previous step.

```
"AzureAd": {
    "Instance": "https://login.microsoftonline.com/",
    "Domain": "domain",
    "TenantId": "tenantId",
    "ClientId": "resourceId"
  }
```

4. Add the Extension method to configure the JWT
    options, as follows.

```
public static class AzureAdServiceCollection
Extensions
{
public static AuthenticationBuilder
AddAzureAdBearer(this AuthenticationBuilder builder)
=> builder.AddAzureAdBearer(_ => { });
public static AuthenticationBuilder
AddAzureAdBearer(this AuthenticationBuilder builder,
Action<AzureAdOptions> configureOptions)
{
builder.Services.Configure(configureOptions);
builder.Services.AddSingleton<IConfigureOptions
<JwtBearerOptions>, ConfigureAzureOptions>();
builder.AddJwtBearer();
return builder;
}
private class ConfigureAzureOptions: IConfigureNamed
Options<JwtBearerOptions>
{
private readonly AzureAdOptions _azureOptions;
public ConfigureAzureOptions(IOptions<AzureAdOptions>
azureOptions)
{
_azureOptions = azureOptions.Value;
}
public void Configure(string name, JwtBearerOptions
options)
```

```
{
options.Audience = _azureOptions.ClientId;
options.Authority = $"{_azureOptions.Instance}{_
azureOptions.TenantId}";
}
public void Configure(JwtBearerOptions options)
{
Configure(Options.DefaultName, options);
}
}
}
```

This code configures the JWT Bearer authentication scheme. The client ID from AppSettings acts as the audience. The AddJwtBearer method is provided by Microsoft.AspNetCore.Authentication.Jwt Bearer. This method automatically downloads the public key based on the tenant ID provided, reads the token in the header, and validates it using public keys. If the validation is successful, claims obtained from the JWT token are added in the user claims context; otherwise, a 401 error is returned.

5.   Add the following code in startup.cs to read the configuration. Call the preceding extension method to pass the configuration.

```
services.AddAuthentication(sharedOptions =>
{
    sharedOptions.DefaultScheme = JwtBearerDefaults.
    AuthenticationScheme;
})
.AddAzureAdBearer(options => Configuration.
Bind("AzureAd", options));
```

6. Add a home controller to emit an index page in
    HTML. Add Reference to ADAL JS Library.

7. Add a value controller to add API methods. These
    API methods are called from JS. Mark these API
    methods with the Authorize attribute, which makes
    sure that only authorized users can access this
    method; unauthorized users get a 401 response.

8. Create an app.js file and store the necessary
    configurations to communicate with Azure AD. Add
    login and logout button handlers, as follows.

```
window.config = {
        instance: 'https://login.microsoftonline.com/',
        tenant: '35d622d5-3f93-42b1-8984-3e2606dbe321',
        clientId: '0170d69b-717f-4164-8185-69c58f9892b8',
        postLogoutRedirectUri: window.location.origin,
        cacheLocation: 'localStorage'
};

var authContext = new AuthenticationContext(config);
// Register NavBar Click Handlers
$signOutButton.click(function () {
authContext.logOut();
});
$signInButton.click(function () {
        authContext.login();
});
```

9. ADAL JS library is responsible for redirecting the
    user to the login page, handling login and logout,
    and managing, storing, and fetching the ID token.

10. Add a home controller in JavaScript. On request, it
     acquires a token from Azure AD and sends a request
     to the value controller by adding a bearer ID token
     in the header. Please refer to the following code to
     acquire a token and send the request to the value
     controller.

```javascript
$("#ViewData").click(function (event) {
        clearErrorMessage();

        // Acquire Token for Backend
        authContext.acquireToken(authContext.config.
        clientId, function (error, token)  {

            // Handle ADAL Errors
            if (error || !token) {
                printErrorMessage('ADAL Error
                Occurred: ' + error);
                return;
            }
            // Get values
            $.ajax({
                type: "GET",
                url: "/api/Values",
                headers: {
                    'Authorization': 'Bearer ' +
                    token
                }
            }).done(function (data) {
                $("#lblData").text("values returned
                from API are: " + data[0] + ", " +
                data[1]);
                console.log('Get Call Sucessfull');
```

```
    }).fail(function () {
        console.log('Fail to get values');
        printErrorMessage('Error in Getting
        Values');
    });
  });
});
```

If you face any difficulty with these steps, please download the code from the GitHub repository at https://github.com/aadfordevelopers/AadDemos/tree/master/SinglePageApplication.

To run the sample code, download it from GitHub and add the configuration to the code. Follow these steps to add the configuration.

1. Open web.config from the downloaded sample.

2. Add a tenant ID, which was obtained in the previous step.

3. Add a client ID in the audience field.

4. Open the app and go to Scripts ➤ App.js ➤ windows.config.

5. Add a tenant and a client ID to the windows.config section.

Your sample is ready to run. Press F5. You are redirected to the index page, as shown in Figure 3-2.

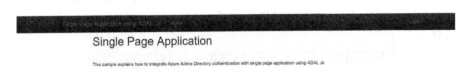

Figure 3-2. Sample home page

Click the Login button. You are redirected to the login page. Log in with your account. After successful validation, the ID token is received and saved in local storage. The Login button is hidden, and the Logout button appears. When you are logged in, your user email address is displayed in the header, as shown in Figure 3-3.

Figure 3-3. *Sample home page after logging in*

Click the Home Page button. You then see a Get Data button. Click this button, and the Azure AD library will read the ID token from local storage and send a request to the Web API controller with a bearer ID token in the authorization header. The API validates the token and returns the data, which is shown on the screen, as seen in Figure 3-4.

Figure 3-4. *Sample home page showing the Get Data button*

In this section, you learned about authenticating a single-page application and calling its own API using Azure Active Directory and ADAL JS.

Now let's look at how you can call a different API from a single-page application. To do this, we will extend the same application, but there is a slight change in the sequence diagram, as shown in Figure 3-5.

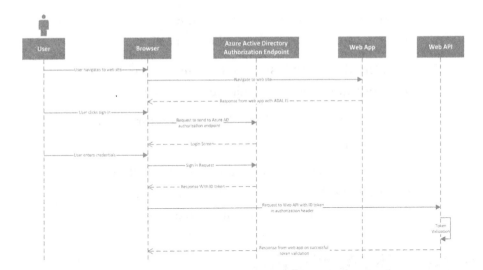

Figure 3-5. *Sequence diagram for single-page application authentication with a different API*

The following sequence of events are performed during authentication.

1. The user navigates to the web application.

2. The web application redirects the user to the login page provided by Azure AD.

3. The user enters credentials and submits the sign-in request to the Azure Active Directory authorization endpoint.

4. On successful validation of the credentials, the Azure AD authorization endpoint returns the authorization code.

5. The web app requests the request bearer access token and the refresh token from the Azure AD token endpoint using the authorization code. After receiving the tokens, the web app caches the tokens in the user session.

6. The request with an access token in the authorization header is sent to the Web API.

7. The Web API, which is secured by Azure Active Directory authentication, validates the token.

8. On successful validation, the response is returned to the web app.

9. If the access token is expired, the web app sends a request to the Azure AD token endpoint to fetch a new access token by using a refresh token.

Running the Application

The first step is to register a new Web API application on Azure AD.

1. Create a new app in the Azure AD app registration by following the same steps you followed for the web app.

2. Note the application ID. It acts as a resource ID in single-page applications and as a client ID in the Web API.

3. To communicate with the Web API, a single-page app in Azure AD should delegate access to the new Web API app. To do this, follow these steps.

    a. Go to the single-page application app in Azure Active Directory apps.

    b. Go to API Permission ➤ Add a Permission. Select an API.

    c. Search the newly added Web API and select the user impersonation permission.

    d. Grant admin consent by clicking the Grant Admin Consent button.

Adding a Web API

To create a Web API, follow these steps.

1. Create a Web API MVC application using .NET Core 2.0.

2. Install the Microsoft.IdentityModel.Clients.

   ActiveDirectory package from NuGet (www.nuget.org).

3. Move the following code snippets from the single-page application to the Web API.

   a. AzureAdOptions

   b. AzureAdOptions configuration from appsettings.json

   c. Extension method for JWT Bearer authentication

   d. Code snippet in startup file

   e. Value controller

4. Add the client ID and tenant ID in appsettings.json.

5. Update the configuration in app.js to add the resource for the Web API, as follows.

```
window.config = {
        instance: 'https://login.microsoftonline.com/',
        tenant: '35d622d5-3f93-42b1-8984-3e2606dbe321',
        resourceId: 'bd5c52b2-8d57-4a67-b371-298c023c95a8',
        clientId: '0170d69b-717f-4164-8185-69c58f9892b8',
        postLogoutRedirectUri: window.location.origin,
        cacheLocation: 'localStorage'
    };
```

If you face any difficulty in following these steps, please download the code from the GitHub repository at

https://github.com/aadfordevelopers/AadDemos/tree/master/
SinglePageApplicationWithAPI.

Update the sample with the configuration, as shown. Your sample is
ready to run. Press F5. Everything is the same as in the previous demo,
except the response comes from the newly added Web API. Make sure that
both projects are marked as a startup project.

Note   Calling a cross-origin API from a JavaScript client is not a
recommended approach. If there is a need to call an external API,
rather than calling the external API directly from JavaScript, it should
be called via the web app using the *on-behalf-of* flow, which is
explained later in this chapter.

Web App/Web API Authentication

In the context of this book, a web app refers to a .NET Core 2.1 web
application, and a Web API refers to the .NET Core 2.1 Web API. The Azure
Active Directory Authentication Library (ADAL) uses the OpenID Connect
OAuth 2 code grant flow to authenticate web apps and the Web API.

The code grant flow was explained in Chapter 2 in the context of native
apps/Web API authentication. With a web app, the user is authenticated by
providing credentials, and in return, the web app receives authentication
code from Azure AD. The authentication code fetches the access and
refresh tokens for the Web API. Both the access token and the refresh
token are cached in the user session (in memory or distributed cache).
Whenever there is a need to call the Web API, the access token is fetched
from the cache; if it has expired, then the access token is refreshed using
the refresh token from Azure AD. The diagram in Figure 3-6 shows the
sequence of events that happen when authenticating a web app/Web API
using Azure Active Directory.

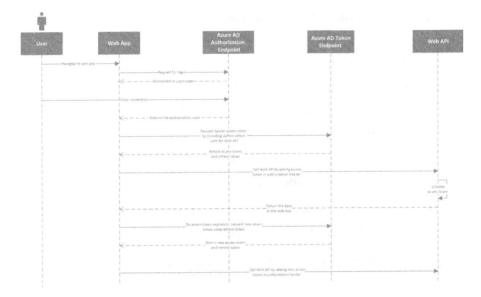

Figure 3-6. *Sequence diagram for web app/Web API
authentication*

The following sequence of events are performed during
authentication.

1. The user navigates to the web application.

2. The web application redirects the user to the login
    page provided by Azure AD.

3. The user clicks the sign-in button or performs a
    secure operation.

4. The user is redirected to the login page.

5. The user enters credentials and submits the sign-in
    request to the Azure Active Directory authorization
    endpoint.

6. On successful validation of the credentials, the Azure AD authorization endpoint returns the authorization code.

7. A request for a bearer access token and a refresh token are sent to the Azure AD token endpoint using an authorization code.

8. The request with an access token in the authorization header is sent to the Web API.

9. The Web API, which is secured by Azure Active Directory authentication, validates the token.

10. On successful validation, a response is returned.

Running the Application

The prerequisites are the same as those for the previous demonstrations. The first step is to register both the web app and the Web API application with Azure AD and fill in the configurations accordingly. The following is a step-by-step demonstration of registering a Web API application with Azure AD.

1. Go to `https://portal.azure.com`.

2. Go to Azure Active Directory in the left navigation pane.

3. Click App Registrations.

4. Click New Registration.

5. Enter the name of your application, which can be changed later.

6. Enter **https://localhost:44364** as the redirect URL, and choose Web in the drop-down menu.

7. Click Register.

8. Copy the application ID. It is the client ID for your application and required for token validation.

9. Grant permissions to your application in API Permission and click the Grant Admin Consent button. Click Yes to confirm.

Here is a step-by-step demonstration of registering a web app with Azure AD.

1. Go to `https://portal.azure.com`.

2. Go to Azure Active Directory from the left navigation pane.

3. Click App Registrations.

4. Click New Registration.

5. Enter the name of your application, which can be changed later.

6. Enter **`https://localhost:44351/`** as the redirect URL, and choose Web in the drop-down menu.

7. Click Register.

8. Copy the application ID. It is the client ID for your application and required for authentication.

9. Go to API Permission ➤ Add a Permission. Select an API.

10. Search the newly added Web API and select the user impersonation permission.

11. Grant admin consent by clicking the Grant Admin Consent button.

12. Generate a client secret. Go to Certificate and Secrets ➤ New Client Secret ➤ Give Description and Duration. Click Add. Copy the key and save it in a secured place. This key is no longer visible after you close the tile.

The configurations are ready. The next step is to create the web app and the Web API and enable Azure Active Directory authentication for it.

Creating a Web App

Follow these steps to create a web app.

1. Create a web app MVC application using .NET Core 2.0 with the default template.

2. Install the Microsoft.IdentityModel.Clients. ActiveDirectory package from NuGet (www.nuget. org).

3. Add the AzureAdOptions class to read the config, as shown the following format.

```
public class AzureAdOptions
    {
        public string ClientId { get; set; }

        public string ClientSecret { get; set; }

        public string Instance { get; set; }

        public string Domain { get; set; }

        public string TenantId { get; set; }

        public string CallbackPath { get; set; }
```

```csharp
    public string Authority
    {
        get
        {
            return $"{Instance}{TenantId}";
        }
    }
    public string ResourceId { get; set; }

    public string APIBaseAddress { get; set; }

    public static AzureAdOptions Settings { set;
    get; }
}
```

4. Add the configurations to appsettings.json in the
    following format. Fill in the configuration values as
    per the registration done in the previous step.

```json
"AzureAd": {
        // Coordinates of the Azure AD Tenant
        "Instance": "https://login.microsoftonline.com/",
        "Domain": "mohitgargoutlook.onmicrosoft.com",
        "TenantId": "35d622d5-3f93-42b1-8984-
                    3e2606dbe321",

        // Coordinates of the Web app
        "ClientId": "7d2c3ba9-3058-4b56-967c-
        5ad77b6241fa",
        "CallbackPath": "/signin-oidc",
        "ClientSecret": "1HJih5gw6fIsfM93NG/
                    IIA6pqdSZbeTcum8qCtPcWaA=",
```

```
              // Coordinates of the Web API
              "ResourceId": "c6b7b3ff-80c6-45f6-aa97-5f70ff89
                            65d9", // ClientId of the Web API
              "APIBaseAddress": "https://localhost:44300"
          }
```

5. Add the TokenSessionCache class and inherit this
    class from the token cache. The TokenSessionCache
    class provides methods to store user-related access
    and refresh tokens in the user session and to clear
    all the tokens at logout or session expiry. Please refer
    to the following code.

```
public class TokenSessionCache : TokenCache
{
    private static readonly object FileLock = new
    object();
    string UserObjectId = string.Empty;
    string CacheId = string.Empty;
    ISession Session = null;

    public TokenSessionCache(string userId,
    ISession session)
    {
        UserObjectId = userId;
        CacheId = UserObjectId + "_TokenCache";
        Session = session;
        this.AfterAccess = AfterAccessNotification;
        this.BeforeAccess = BeforeAccessNotification;
        Load();
    }
```

```csharp
public void Load()
{
    lock (FileLock)
    {
        this.Deserialize(Session.Get(CacheId));
    }
}

public void Persist()
{
    lock (FileLock)
    {
        // reflect changes in the persistent store
        Session.Set(CacheId, this.Serialize());
        // once the write operation took place,
            restore the HasStateChanged bit to false
        this.HasStateChanged = false;
    }
}

// Empties the persistent store.
public override void Clear()
{
    base.Clear();
    Session.Remove(CacheId);
}
```

```
public override void DeleteItem(TokenCacheItem item)
    {
        base.DeleteItem(item);
        Persist();
    }

// Triggered right before ADAL needs to access the
    cache.
// Reload the cache from the persistent store in
    case it changed since the last access.
void BeforeAccessNotification(TokenCacheNotificati
onArgs args)
    {
        Load();
    }
// Triggered right after ADAL accessed the cache.
void AfterAccessNotification(TokenCache
NotificationArgs args)
    {
        // if the access operation resulted in a cache
            update
        if (this.HasStateChanged)
        {
            Persist();
        }
    }
}
```

6. Add the Extension method to configure the web app
   authentication.

```
public static AuthenticationBuilder AddAzureAd(this
AuthenticationBuilder builder, Action<AzureAdOptions>
configureOptions)
        {
            builder.Services.Configure(configureOptions);
            builder.Services.AddSingleton<IConfigure
            Options<OpenIdConnectOptions>,
            ConfigureAzureOptions>();
            builder.AddOpenIdConnect();
            return builder;
        }
```

7. Define ConfigureAzureOptions as follows to assign
    the configuration.

```
private class ConfigureAzureOptions : IConfigureNamedO
ptions<OpenIdConnectOptions>
        {
            private readonly AzureAdOptions _
            azureOptions;

            public ConfigureAzureOptions(IOptions
            <AzureAdOptions> azureOptions)
            {
                _azureOptions = azureOptions.Value;
            }

            public void Configure(string name,
            OpenIdConnectOptions options)
            {
                options.ClientId = _azureOptions.
                ClientId;
                options.Authority = _azureOptions.
                Authority;
```

```
            options.UseTokenLifetime = true;
            options.CallbackPath = _azureOptions.
            CallbackPath;
             options.RequireHttpsMetadata = false;
            options.ClientSecret = _azureOptions.
            ClientSecret;
             options.Resource = _azureOptions.
             ResourceId;
            options.ResponseType = "id_token code";

            // Subscribing to the OIDC events
            options.Events.
            OnAuthorizationCodeReceived =
            OnAuthorizationCodeReceived;
        }

        public void Configure(OpenIdConnectOptions
        options)
        {
            Configure(Options.DefaultName, options);
        }
    }
```

8. The Response type default value is ID_token,
   which means it will only call the OnTokenValidated
   event. Override the value of the response code
   to id_token_code. This means it will call the
   OnAuthorizationCodeReceived event after the
   OnTokenValidated event, which makes sure
   Context.Principal has a value before calling
   AuthorizationCodeReceived.

9. Define the OnAuthorizationCodeReceived method
    as follows.

```
private async Task OnAuthorizationCodeReceived
(AuthorizationCodeReceivedContext context)
            {
                    string userObjectId = (context.
                    Principal.FindFirst("http://schemas.
                    microsoft.com/identity/claims/
                    objectidentifier"))?.Value;
                    var authContext = new Authentication
                    Context(context.Options.Authority,
                    new TokenSessionCache(userObjectId,
                    context.HttpContext.Session));
                    var credential = new ClientCredential
                    (context.Options.ClientId, context.
                    Options.ClientSecret);

                    var authResult = await authContext.
                    AcquireTokenByAuthorizationCodeAsync
                    (context.TokenEndpointRequest.Code,
                        new Uri(context.TokenEndpoint
                        Request.RedirectUri, UriKind.
                        RelativeOrAbsolute), credential,
                        context.Options.Resource);

                    // Notify the OIDC middleware that
                        we already took care of code
                        redemption.
                    context.HandleCodeRedemption
                    (authResult.AccessToken, context.
                    ProtocolMessage.IdToken);
            }
```

10. Call the AddAzureAd extension method in the startup file as follows to configure the authentication.

```
services.AddAuthentication(sharedOptions =>
    {
        sharedOptions.DefaultScheme = Cookie
        AuthenticationDefaults.AuthenticationScheme;
        sharedOptions.DefaultChallengeScheme =
        OpenIdConnectDefaults.AuthenticationScheme;
    })
    .AddAzureAd(options =>
    {
        Configuration.Bind("AzureAd", options);
        AzureAdOptions.Settings = options;
    })
    .AddCookie();
```

11. By default, a session stores all the data in the memory cache. Storing an access token in the memory cache is never recommended. As in case of server restart, memory cache will not persist. Also in case of load balancer scenario's, memory cache will not be replicated across servers. Absence of memory cache will ask user again for login. To avoid frequent login, the session should be stored in a distributed cache like Redis or a database like SQL Server.

The SQL Server distributed cache can be configured without writing any additional code. To configure the SQL Server cache, add the following lines of code in startup.

```
services.AddDistributedSqlServerCache(options =>
        {
            options.ConnectionString =
                _config["ConnectionString"];
            options.SchemaName = "dbo";
            options.TableName = "TestCache";
        });
```

12. Add an account controller and add methods to
    handle sign-in and sign-out requests and redirect
    the user to the signed-out and access-denied pages.

    a. **Sign-in**. The following code redirects the user to the sign-in
       page.

    ```
    var redirectUrl = Url.Action(nameof(HomeController.
    Index), "Home");
                return Challenge(
                        new AuthenticationProperties { Redirect
                        Uri = redirectUrl, AllowRefresh = true },
                        OpenIdConnectDefaults.Authentication
                        Scheme);
    ```

    b. **Sign out.** Adds a sign-out method that removes all cached
       entries for the user and sends an OpenID Connect sign-out
       request.

    ```
    string userObjectID = User.FindFirst("http://
    schemas.microsoft.com/identity/claims/
    objectidentifier").Value;
                var authContext = new AuthenticationCont
                ext(AzureAdOptions.Settings.Authority,
                new TokenSessionCache(userObjectID,
                HttpContext.Session));
    ```

```
authContext.TokenCache.Clear();

// Let Azure AD sign-out
var callbackUrl = Url.
Action(nameof(SignedOut), "Account",
values: null, protocol: Request.Scheme);
return SignOut(
    new AuthenticationProperties
    { RedirectUri = callbackUrl,
    AllowRefresh = true },
    CookieAuthenticationDefaults.
    AuthenticationScheme,
    OpenIdConnectDefaults.Authentication
    Scheme);
```

c. **Signed out.** Redirects the user to a signed-out view if the user is not authenticated. Adds a view with HTML to show a signed-out message.

```
If (User.Identity.IsAuthenticated)
    {
        // Redirect to home page if the user
            is authenticated.
        return RedirectToAction(nameof
        (HomeController.Index), "Home");
    }

    return View();
```

d. **Access Denied.** Adds a method to redirect the user to an access-denied view if the user doesn't have access to the requested resource.

13. Adds a controller to send a request to the API. To
     send the request, add an access token in the
     authorization header of the HTTP request. An
     access token is fetched from the user session, and
     if the access token has expired, an access token is
     fetched from Azure AD by using a refresh token. If
     both tokens are expired, then the user is redirected
     to the login page. Please refer to the following code.

```
string userObjectID = (User.FindFirst("http://schemas.
microsoft.com/identity/claims/objectidentifier"))?.Value;

                    AuthenticationContext authContext
                    = new AuthenticationContext(Azure
                    AdOptions.Settings.Authority, new
                    TokenSessionCache(userObjectID,
                    HttpContext.Session));

                    ClientCredential credential = new
                    ClientCredential(AzureAdOptions.
                    Settings.ClientId, AzureAdOptions.
                    Settings.ClientSecret);

                    result = await authContext.Acquir
                    eTokenSilentAsync(AzureAdOptions.
                    Settings.ResourceId, credential,
                    new UserIdentifier(userObjectID,
                    UserIdentifierType.UniqueId));
```

Put this code block in Try Block to catch the
exception. The code fetches the token from the
cache or from Azure AD, depending on the expiry
status. If both tokens are expired, then it raises an
exception. The following code redirects the user to
the login page.

```
catch (Exception ex)
        {
            if (HttpContext.Request.Query["reauth"]
            == "True")
            {
                // If Reauth is required challenge
                for login again
                return new ChallengeResult
                (OpenIdConnectDefaults.
                AuthenticationScheme);
            }
        }
```

Creating a Web API

After creating the web app, follow these steps to create the Web API.

1. Create a Web API MVC application using .NET Core 2.0.

2. Install the Microsoft.IdentityModel.Clients. ActiveDirectory package from NuGet (www.nuget.org).

3. Add the AzureAdOptions class to read the config, as shown in the following format.

```
public class AzureAdOptions
    {
public string ClientId { get; set; }
public string ClientSecret { get; set; }
public string Instance { get; set; }
public string Domain { get; set; }
public string TenantId { get; set; }
    }
```

4. Add the configuration in appsettings.json in the following format. Fill in the configuration values as per the registration done in the previous step.

```
"AzureAd": {
    "Instance": "https://login.microsoftonline.com/",
    "Domain": "domain",
    "TenantId": "tenantId",
    "ClientId": "resourceId"
  }
```

5. Add the Extension method to configure the JWT options, as follows.

```
    public static class AzureAdServiceCollection
    Extensions
{
public static AuthenticationBuilder
AddAzureAdBearer(this AuthenticationBuilder builder)
=> builder.AddAzureAdBearer(_ => { });
public static AuthenticationBuilder
AddAzureAdBearer(this AuthenticationBuilder builder,
Action<AzureAdOptions> configureOptions)
{
builder.Services.Configure(configureOptions);
builder.Services.AddSingleton<IConfigureOptions
<JwtBearerOptions>, ConfigureAzureOptions>();
builder.AddJwtBearer();
return builder;
}
private class ConfigureAzureOptions: IConfigureNamed
Options<JwtBearerOptions>
```

```
{
private readonly AzureAdOptions _azureOptions;
public ConfigureAzureOptions(IOptions<AzureAdOptions>
azureOptions)
{
_azureOptions = azureOptions.Value;
}
public void Configure(string name, JwtBearerOptions
options)
{
options.Audience = _azureOptions.ClientId;
options.Authority = $"{_azureOptions.Instance}{
_azureOptions.TenantId}";
}
public void Configure(JwtBearerOptions options)
{
Configure(Options.DefaultName, options);
}
}
}
```

This code configures the JWT Bearer authentication
scheme. The client ID from AppSettings acts as the
audience. The AddJwtBearer method is provided by
Microsoft.AspNetCore.Authentication.JwtBearer.
This method automatically downloads the public
key based on the tenant ID provided, reads the
token in the header, and validates it using public
keys. If the validation is successful, then claims
obtained from the JWT token are added in the user
claims context; otherwise, a 401 error is returned.

6. Add the following code in startup.cs to read the configuration and call the preceding extension method to pass the configuration.

```
services.AddAuthentication(sharedOptions =>
{
        sharedOptions.DefaultScheme = JwtBearer
        Defaults.AuthenticationScheme;
})
.AddAzureAdBearer(options => Configuration.Bind
("AzureAd", options));
```

Your Web API is now secured by Azure AD. Add a controller and expose a Web API method.

If you face any difficulty in following these steps, please download the code from the GitHub repository at https://github.com/aadfordevelopers/AadDemos/tree/master/WebApp-WebAPI.

To run the sample code, download it from GitHub and add the configuration in the code. Follow these steps to add the configuration.

1. Open the web app's appsettings.json from the downloaded sample.

2. Add the tenant ID, client ID, and client secret, which were generated in the previous step.

3. Add the Web API's client ID as a resource ID.

4. Open the Web API's appsettings.json from the downloaded sample.

5. Add the tenant ID and client ID to the Web API, which were obtained in the previous step.

Now your sample is ready to run. Press F5. You will be redirected to the index page. Make sure that both projects are marked as the startup projects. Figure 3-7 shows the Home screen in the browser.

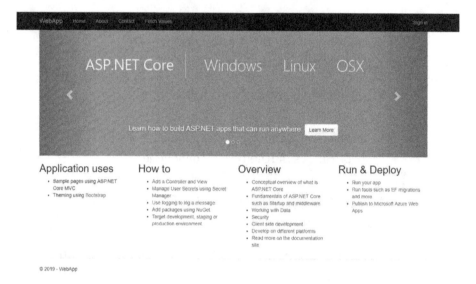

Figure 3-7. *Home screen*

Click the Login button. You are redirected to the login page. Log in with your account. After successful authentication, the web app receives the authentication code. With the help of the authentication code, the ID token, access token, and refresh token are generated and saved in the user session on the server. The Login button is hidden, and the Logout button appears. When you are logged in, your user email address is displayed in the header, as shown in Figure 3-8.

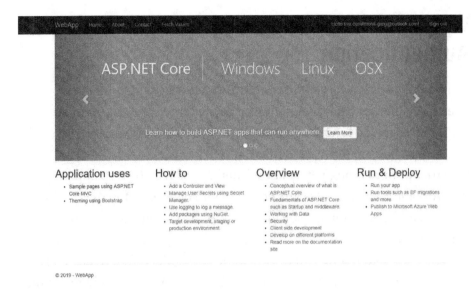

Figure 3-8. *Home screen after login*

Click the Fetch Values tab. The request goes to the web app controller and verifies whether the user is authenticated. If not, the user is directed to the Login page. If the user is successfully authenticated, then the Azure AD library reads the access token from the cache and verifies whether the token is valid. If it is not valid, then the token is refreshed using the refresh token. A valid access token is added in the authentication header and the HTTP call is sent to the API. The API validates the token and returns the data, which is shown on the screen (see Figure 3-9).

Figure 3-9. *Data returned from the API*

Web App: HTTP Triggered Azure Function Authentication

Azure Functions is a serverless compute that is triggered by an event. There are different types of functions provided by Azure. One of them is the HTTP triggered function in Azure, which acts as a serverless API.

To authenticate the Azure Function HTTP triggered function is a little tricky but not tough. It can be authenticated like the web app/ Web API authentication. OAuth 2 code grant flow using OpenID Connect authentication is used for web app/HTTP triggered function authentication.

The user is authenticated by providing credentials, and in return, the web app receives authentication code from Azure AD. The authentication code fetches the access and refresh tokens for Azure Function. Both the access token and the refresh token are cached in the user session (in memory or distributed cache). Whenever there is a need to call Azure Function, the access token is fetched from the cache; if it has expired, then it is refreshed by using the refresh token from Azure AD.

Figure 3-10 is a diagram showing the sequence of events that happen when authenticating a web app/HTTP triggered function using Azure Active Directory.

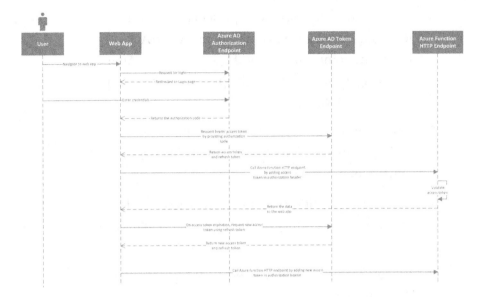

Figure 3-10. *Sequence diagram for web app: HTTP triggered Azure function authentication*

The following sequence of events are performed during authentication.

1. The user navigates to the web application.

2. The web application redirects the user to the Login page provided by Azure AD.

3. The user enters credentials and submits the sign-in request to the Azure Active Directory authorization endpoint.

4. On successful validation of the credentials, the Azure AD authorization endpoint returns the authorization code.

5. The web app requests the request bearer access token and the refresh token from the Azure AD token endpoint using the authorization code. After receiving the tokens, the web app caches the tokens in the user session.

6. The request with an access token in the authorization header is sent to the HTTP triggered Azure function endpoint.

7. The Azure Function endpoint, which is secured by Azure Active Directory authentication, validates the token.

8. On successful validation, a response is returned to the web app.

9. If the access token has expired, the web app sends a request to the Azure AD token endpoint to fetch a new access token by using a refresh token.

Running the Application

The prerequisites are the same as in previous demonstrations. The first step is to register both the web app and the Azure AD Function application with Azure AD and fill in the configurations accordingly. The following is a step-by-step demonstration of registering the HTTP triggered Azure Function app with Azure AD.

1. Go to `https://portal.azure.com`.

2. Go to Azure Active Directory in the left navigation pane.

3. Click App Registrations.

4. Click New Registration.

5. Enter the name of your application, which can be changed later.

6. Enter **https://localhost:44364** as the redirect URL, and choose Web in the drop-down menu.

7. Click Register.

8. Copy the application ID. It is the client ID for your application and required for token validation.

9. Grant permissions to your application in API Permission. Click the Grant Admin Consent button. Click Yes to confirm.

Here is the step-by-step demonstration of registering the web app with Azure AD.

1. Go to https://portal.azure.com.

2. Go to Azure Active Directory in the left navigation pane.

3. Click App Registrations.

4. Click New Registration.

5. Enter the name of your application, which can be changed later.

6. Enter **https://localhost:44351/** as the redirect URL, and choose Web in the drop-down menu.

7. Click Register.

8. Copy the application ID. It is the client ID for your application and required for authentication.

9. Go to API Permission ➤ Add a Permission. Select an API.

10. Search the newly added HTTP triggered Azure
     Function app and select the user impersonation
     permission.

11. Grant admin consent by clicking the Grant Admin
     Consent button.

12. Generate a client secret. Go to Certificate and
     Secrets ➤ New Client Secret ➤ Give Description
     and Duration. Click Add. Copy the key and save it
     in a secured place. This key is not visible again after
     you close the tile.

The configurations are ready. The next step is to create a web app and
the HTTP triggered Azure function and enable Azure Active Directory
authentication for it.

Creating a Web App

Refer to the previous section to create a web app.

Creating an HTTP Triggered Azure Function

The next step is to create an HTTP triggered Azure function endpoint.

1. Go to `http://portal.azure.com`.

2. Create the Function app with default options. Make
    sure the runtime stack is .NET.

3. In the Azure Function app, add the HTTP triggered
    Azure function.

4. Use the same default C# code that is already there.
    Only change the object result to $"Hello, {name}.
    This is the response from Azure Function."

5. Note the Azure AD Function app URL by clicking the Get Function URL link.

Figure 3-11. *Authorization screen for HTTP triggered Azure function*

6. Click Integrate. In the "Authorization level" menu, select Anonymous (see Figure 3-11).

7. Go to the Function app. Select the platform features, and then select Authentication/Authorization.

8. Enable App Service Authentication.

9. Choose Azure Active Directory as the authentication provider. Refer to Figure 3-12.

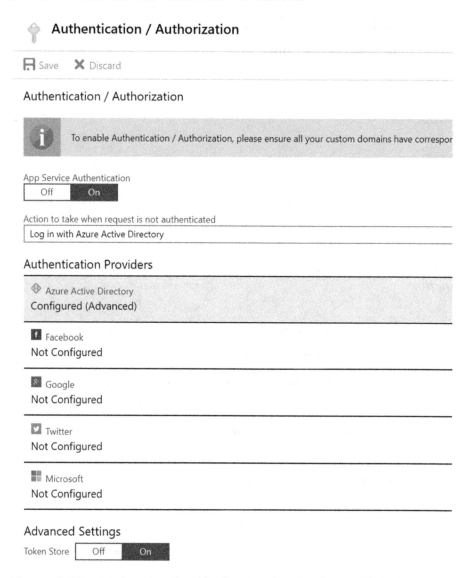

Figure 3-12. *Authentication/Authorization for Azure Function*

10. Add the client ID, which generated in a previous step, when registering the Azure Function app with Azure AD.

11. Add the issuer URL as `https://login.windows.net/{tenantId}`.

12. In the "Action to take when the request is not authenticated" drop-down menu, select "Log in with Azure Active Directory".

13. Click Save. Refer to Figure 3-13.

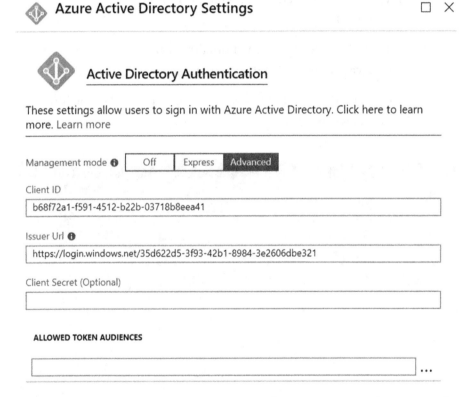

Figure 3-13. Azure Active Directory authentication configuration for Azure Function

If you face any difficulty in following these steps, please download the code from the GitHub repository at `https://github.com/aadfordevelopers/AadDemos/tree/master/WebApp-FunctionAPI`.

To run the sample code, download it from GitHub and add the configuration in the code. Follow these steps to add the configuration.

1. Open the web app's appsettings.json from the downloaded sample.

2. Add the tenant ID, client ID, and client secret, which were generated in the previous step.

3. Add the Azure Function app's client ID as the resource ID.

4. Add APIBaseAddress as the Function app URL, which was generated in the previous step.

The sample is ready to run. Press F5. You are redirected to the index page, as shown in Figure 3-14.

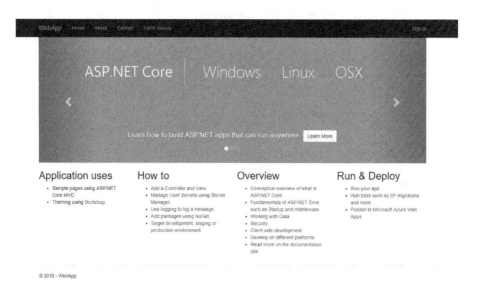

Figure 3-14. *Web app index page*

Click the Login button. You are redirected to the Login page. Log in with your account. After successful authentication, the web app receives the authentication code. With the help of the authentication code, the ID token, access token, and refresh token are generated and saved in the user session on the server. The Login button is hidden, and the Logout button appears. When you are logged in, your user email address is displayed in the header, as shown in Figure 3-15.

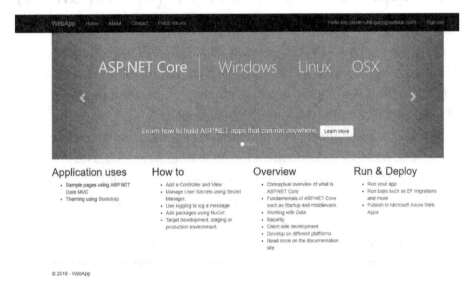

Figure 3-15. *Web app screen after login*

Click the Fetch Values tab. The request goes to the web app controller and verifies whether the user is authenticated. If not, the user is directed to the Login page. If the user is successfully authenticated, then the Azure AD library reads the access token from the cache and verifies whether the token is valid. If it is not valid, then the token is refreshed using a refresh token. A valid access token is added to the authentication header. The HTTP call is sent to the HTTP triggered Azure function endpoint. Azure Function validates the token and returns the data, which is shown on the screen (see Figure 3-16).

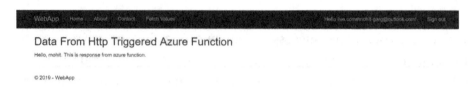

Figure 3-16. *Showing data from Azure Function*

Web App/Web API/Web API 2 (On-Behalf-Of)

This authentication flow is the extension of a code grant flow in which a web app and the Web API is involved. If there is a need to communicate with other APIs (say, Web API 2) from the Web API, then the OAuth 2.0 *on-behalf-of* flow is used. *On-behalf-of* means a request to a second Web API is raised on behalf of the logged-in user identity.

The user is authenticated by providing credentials, and in return, the web app receives an authentication code from Azure AD. The authentication code fetches an access token and a refresh token for the Web API. Both the access token and the refresh token are cached in the user session (in memory or distributed cache). Whenever there is a need to call the Web API access token, it is fetched from the cache; if it has expired, then it is refreshed using a refresh token from Azure AD. After validating the access token, the Web API generates an *on-behalf-of* access token for the second API using user assertion and client credentials. The user assertion contains the username, user access token, and grant type.

Figure 3-17 is a diagram showing the sequence of events that happen when authenticating the *on-behalf-of* flow using Azure Active Directory.

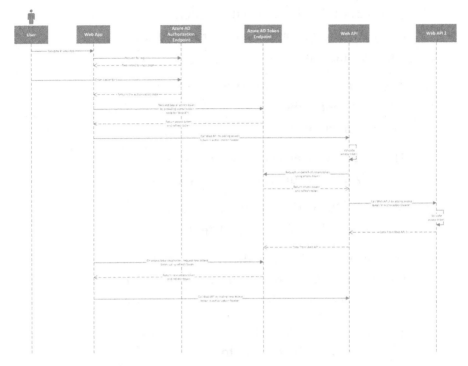

Figure 3-17. *Sequence diagram for on-behalf-of authentication flow*

The following sequence of events are performed during authentication.

1. The user navigates to the web application.

2. The web application redirects the user to the login page provided by Azure AD.

3. The user clicks the sign-in button or performs a secure operation.

4. The user is redirected to the Login page.

5. The user enters credentials and submits the sign-in request to the Azure Active Directory authorization endpoint.

95

6. On successful validation of the credentials, the Azure AD authorization endpoint returns the authorization code.

7. A request for a bearer access token and refresh token are sent to the Azure AD token endpoint using the authorization code.

8. The request with an access token in the authorization header is sent to the Web API.

9. The Web API, which is secured by Azure Active Directory authentication, validates the token.

10. On successful validation, the Web API requests bearer access for Web API 2 using the user assertion and its own credentials.

11. The request with an access token in the authorization header is sent to Web API 2.

12. On successful validation, Web API 2 returns the response.

Running the Application

The prerequisites are the same as in previous demonstrations. The first step is to register the web app, Web API, and Web API 2 with Azure AD and generate the configurations accordingly. The following is a step-by-step demonstration of registering Web API 2 with Azure AD.

1. Go to `https://portal.azure.com`.

2. Go to Azure Active Directory in the left navigation pane.

3. Click App Registrations.

4. Click New Registration.

5. Enter the name of your application, which can be changed later.

6. Enter **https://localhost:44364** as the redirect URL, and choose Web in the drop-down menu.

7. Click Register.

8. Copy the application ID. It is the client ID for your application and required for token validation.

Here is a step-by-step demonstration of registering the Web API with Azure AD.

1. Go to https://portal.azure.com.

2. Go to Azure Active Directory in the left navigation pane.

3. Click App Registrations.

4. Click New App Registration.

5. Enter the name of your Web API and select the application type: Web app/API.

6. Enter **https://localhost:44330** as the application URL and click Create.

7. Copy the application ID. It is the client ID for your application and required for token validation.

8. The Web API generates on behalf of the token for Web API 2. So, it should have access to the Web API with admin consent.

9. Go to API Permission ➤ Add a Permission. Select an API.

10. Search the newly added Web API and select the user impersonation permission.

11. Grant admin consent by clicking the Grant Admin Consent button.

12. Generate a client secret. Go to Certificate and Secrets ➤ New Client Secret ➤ Give Description and Duration. Click Add. Copy the key and save it in a secured place. This key is not visible again after you close the tile.

Here is a step-by-step demonstration of registering the web app with Azure AD.

1. Go to `https://portal.azure.com`.

2. Go to Azure Active Directory from the left navigation pane.

3. Click App Registrations.

4. Click New Registration.

5. Enter the name of your application, which can be changed later.

6. Enter **`https://localhost:44351/`** as the redirect URL, and choose Web in the drop-down menu.

7. Click Register.

8. Copy the application ID. It is the client ID for your application and required for authentication.

9. Go to API Permission ➤ Add a Permission. Select an API.

10. Search the newly added Web API. Select the user impersonation permission, because the web app generates an access token for the Web API.

11. Grant admin consent by clicking the Grant Admin Consent button.

12. Generate a client secret. Go to Certificate and Secrets ➤ New Client Secret ➤ Give Description and Duration. Click Add. Copy the key and save it in a secured place. This key is not visible again after you close the tile.

The configurations are ready. The next step is to create a web app, a Web API, and a Web API 2 and enable Azure Active Directory authentication for it.

Creating a Web App and a Web API 2

Refer to the "Web App/Web API 2 Authentication" section to create a web app and Web API 2.

Creating a Web API

To create the Web API 2, follow the same steps in previous demonstrations. Next, make the following changes.

1. Change the Configure method in the static class to change the SaveSigninToken value to true. SaveSigninToken true means the API will store the token in bootstrap context, which is required to generate the *on-behalf-of* access token.

   ```
   public void Configure(string name, JwtBearerOptions options)
   {
   ```

99

```
                options.Audience = _azureOptions.
                ClientId;
                options.Authority = $"{_azureOptions.
                Instance}{_azureOptions.TenantId}";
                options.TokenValidationParameters =
                new TokenValidationParameters() {
                SaveSigninToken = true };
        }
```

2. In the API controller, instead of returning the data,
   call the Web API 2 by adding the *on-behalf-of* token
   in the authorization header and return the response
   from Web API 2. To generate the *on-behalf-of* token,
   use the following code.

```
var userAccessToken = HttpContext.User.Identities.
First().BootstrapContext.ToString();
            var claims = HttpContext.User.Claims;
            string userName = claims.Where(m => m.Type
            == ClaimTypes.Upn).Any() ? claims.First(m =>
            m.Type == ClaimTypes.Upn).Value : claims.
            First(m => m.Type == ClaimTypes.Email).
            Value;
            UserAssertion userAssertion = new
            UserAssertion(userAccessToken,
            "urn:ietf:params:oauth:grant-type:jwt-
            bearer", userName);
            string userObjectID = (User.
            FindFirst("http://schemas.microsoft.com/
            identity/claims/objectidentifier"))?.Value;
            AuthenticationContext authContext = new Aut
            henticationContext(AzureAdOptions.Settings.
            Authority);
```

```
ClientCredential credential = new Client
Credential(AzureAdOptions.Settings.
ClientId, AzureAdOptions.Settings.
ClientSecret);
var result = await authContext.AcquireToke
nAsync(AzureAdOptions.Settings.ResourceId,
credential, userAssertion);
```

This code prepares the user assertion. With the help of user assertion and client credentials, it sends a request to Azure AD to fetch the access token.

If you face any difficulty in following these steps, please download the code from the GitHub repository at `https://github.com/aadfordevelopers/AadDemos/tree/master/WebApp-WebAPI-OnBehalfOf`.

To run the sample code, download it from GitHub and add the configuration to the code. Follow these steps to add the configuration.

1. Open Web API 2 appsettings.json from the downloaded sample.

2. Add the tenant ID and client ID, which were obtained in the previous step.

3. Open Web API appsettings.json from the downloaded sample.

4. Add the tenant ID, client ID, and client secret, which were generated in the previous step.

5. Add the Web API 2 client ID as the resource ID.

6. Open the web app's appsettings.json from the downloaded sample.

7. Add the tenant ID, client ID, and client secret, which were generated in the previous step.

8. Add the Web API client ID as the resource ID.

Your sample is ready to run. Press F5. You are redirected to the index page, which shows up in the browser, as shown in Figure 3-18. Make sure both projects are marked as the startup project.

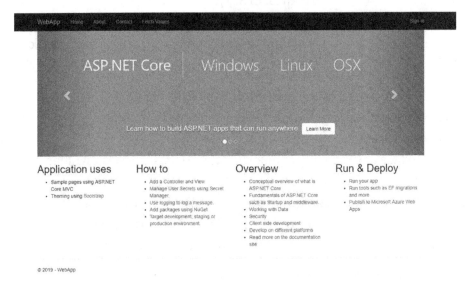

Figure 3-18. *Home screen*

Click the Login button. You are redirected to the Login page. Log in with your account. After successful authentication, the web app receives the authentication code. With the help of the authentication code, the ID token, access token, and refresh token are generated and saved in the user session on the server. The Login button is hidden, and the Logout button appears. When you are logged in, your user email address is displayed in the header, as shown in Figure 3-19.

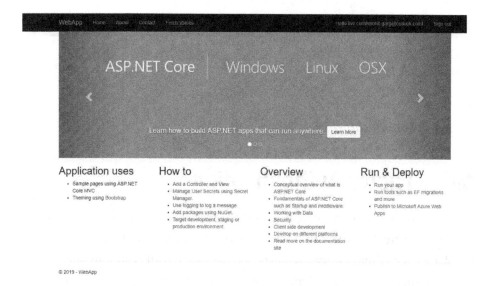

Figure 3-19. *Home Screen showing logged in user*

Click the Fetch Values tab. The request goes to the web app controller and verifies whether the user is authenticated. If not, the user is directed to the Login page. If the user is successfully authenticated, then the Azure AD library reads the access token from the cache and verifies whether the token is valid. If it is not valid, then the token is refreshed using a refresh token. A valid access token is added in the authentication header and the HTTP call is sent to the API. The API validates the token, and on successful validation, the Web API sends the request to the Azure AD authorization endpoint to fetch the access token for Web API 2 by using user assertion. The access token is added to the authorization header. The HTTP call is sent to Web API 2. On successful validation by Web API 2, a response is returned to the Web API and from the Web API to the web app, as shown in Figure 3-20.

Figure 3-20. *Result from API 2*

Multi-Factor Authentication

Multi-factor authentication (MFA) is the most secure and advanced way to authenticate. In addition to your credentials, one or more factors are involved for authentication. None of the factors has any relationship between them; they are independent. Factors like one-time password (OTP), security questions, request approval by an Android or iOS application, or by a phone call and so forth to provide additional security.

The Need for Multi-Factor Authentication

In the world of information technology, cyber attacks are increasing day after day. Therefore, it is essential to save our web apps from security attacks. Single-factor authentication using a username and password for a web app is not enough to secure it from cyber attacks because of following reasons.

- Passwords are easily guessable.

- The same password is used for multiple web sites.

- Password theft.

- Password "remember" features across devices. If the device is compromised, then all the web apps for which a password is secured are compromised automatically.

- Saving all passwords in a single location to refer to whenever required.

- A lot of support is required if the complexity of a password is increased.

- Passwords can be cracked using brute force.

In short, password-based, single-factor authentication is not secure enough to protect a web application from cyber attacks. It may be good for applications that don't require high levels of security, but otherwise, multi-factor authentication is a necessity.

Configuring Multi-Factor Authentication for Azure AD

Microsoft Azure provides multi-factor authentication support for the web applications secured by Azure Active Directory. MFA can only be enabled for Work or School Account users. MFA cannot be enabled for external users because their login policies are managed by their tenant admin.

The following is a step-by-step guide on enabling multi-factor authentication in a web app secured by Azure Active Directory.

1. Go to `http://portal.azure.com`.

2. Go to Azure Active Directory.

3. Click Users in the left navigation tab.

4. Add a new user by using the New User button.

5. Click the Multi-Factor Authentication tab. You will see the screen shown in Figure 3-21.

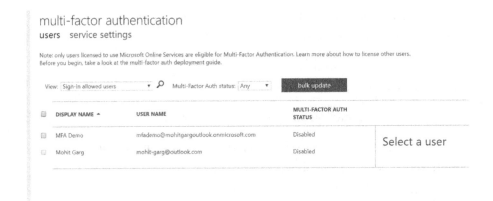

Figure 3-21. *Multi-Factor authentication configuration screen*

6. Select the newly added user (MFA Demo) and click the Enable button to enable multi-factor authentication.

7. After enabling, if you select the same user again, you see a page with Disable, Enforce, and Manage User Settings options, as shown in Figure 3-22.

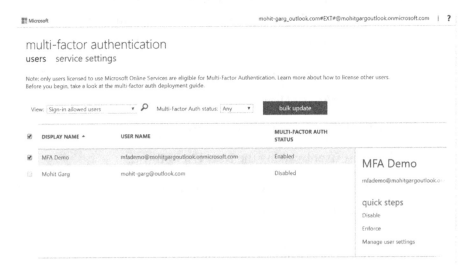

Figure 3-22. *Multi-factor authentication configuration screen*

8. Enable means that MFA is enabled but may or may not be enforced. If the user completed the MFA registration or the admin enforced multi-factor authentication, then only multi-factor authentication is enforced.

9. To change the multi-factor authentication settings, click Service Settings. The settings are shown in Figure 3-23.

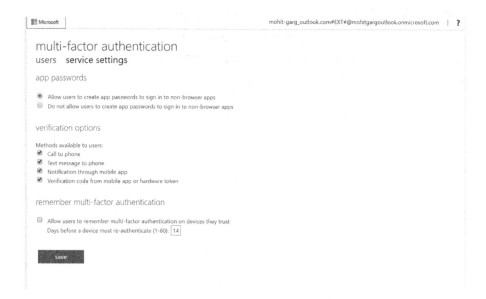

Figure 3-23. *Multi-factor authentication Settings screen*

Enabling multi-factor authentication for Azure AD users is super easy and doesn't take much time. It enhances the security of your authentication to a great extent. It is always preferable to enable multi-factor authentication.

Summary

This chapter discussed how to enable Azure AD authentication for different types of web applications. We started by authenticating single-page applications using implicit flow, and then moved to web app/Web API authentication using code grant flow and API/API 2 authentication using *on-behalf-of* flow. We also covered how Azure Function is used as an HTTP endpoint and how to enable Azure AD authentication for an HTTP triggered Azure Function endpoint.

We discussed why multi-factor authentication is required and how we can enable users who belong to our Active Directory.

Now let's move on to user authentication for native apps, such as a console application, WPF, UWP, or Android.

CHAPTER 4

User-Based Authentication for Native Applications

In Chapter 3, we discussed user authentication on web applications in detail. In this chapter, we focus on user-based authentication for native applications by using the authentication flows and OpenID Connect concepts explained in Chapter 2.

Applications that are designed to run on a specific platform or device are known as *native applications*. In today's constantly evolving world, a lot of devices run on different operating systems. The most popular operating systems are Windows, Android, and iOS. Microsoft Azure AD supports authentication for all the apps built on these operating systems: console, Windows Presentation Foundation, Universal Windows Platform for Windows, Android apps for Android, and iOS apps for the iPhone OS. In this chapter, we cover authentication for the following types of native applications.

- Windows console application: Web API

- Windows Presentation Foundation (WPF): Web API

© Manas Mayank and Mohit Garg 2019
M. Mayank and M. Garg, *Developing Applications with Azure Active Directory*,
https://doi.org/10.1007/978-1-4842-5040-2_4

- Universal Windows Platform (UWP): Azure Function HTTP endpoint

- Android: Azure Function HTTP endpoint

Authentication Using Code Grant Flow

To authenticate native applications, Microsoft Azure AD uses the authorization code grant flow specified in the OAuth 2.0 protocol. Code grant flow was discussed in Chapter 2. Now we will focus on how native apps can be authenticated by using code grant flow.

When running the native app and doing a secure operation, the user is redirected to a web-based login pop-up window, in which the user enters her credentials. On successful validation of the credentials, the native application receives an authentication code. With the authentication code, the access token and refresh token are fetched from the Azure AD authorization endpoint. The access token connects the Web APIs secured by Azure AD.

Figure 4-1 is a diagram showing the sequence of events that happen when authenticating native applications using Azure Active Directory.

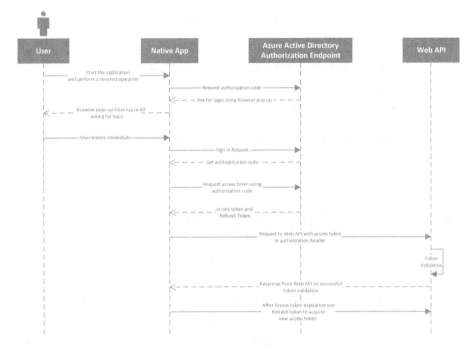

Figure 4-1. *Sequence diagram for native app authentication*

The following events are performed during authentication.

1. The user runs the native application.

2. A request for authorization code is sent to Azure AD.

3. The user is redirected to a browser pop-up window asking for credentials.

4. After the user logs in and the credentials are successfully validated, Azure AD returns the access token and the refresh token.

5. A request with an access token in the authorization header is sent to the Web API.

6. The Web API is secured by Azure Active Directory authentication, which validates the token.

7. On successful validation, a response is returned to the native app.

8. If the access token has expired, the native app sends a request to the Azure AD token endpoint to fetch a new access token through the refresh token.

Now let's move to authenticating native applications through using the protocol flow.

Windows Console Application

A console application is a Windows program that runs on a command prompt via a command-line user interface. Today, most console applications are designed to need no user interaction, like a background process. Azure WebJobs are developed on top of console applications only. There are some applications designed to need little user interaction. There are certain scenarios where we need a little user interaction.

To install certificates on a developer's machine, for example, there are one-click executables that install all the required certificates kept in a key vault. The user only needs to run that executable and log in using their credentials. After successful verification, certificates are downloaded and installed automatically.

There are other scenarios in which user validation should be done before executing the console app. To achieve this, Azure AD provides authentication for console applications.

Running the Application

To develop a Windows console application using Azure Active Directory authentication, you need the following software and completed prerequisites.

- Visual Studio 2017 (If you don't have a license, you can use the Community edition.)

- .NET Core 2.1 SDK

- an Azure subscription and Azure AD tenant

- a user account in your Azure AD tenant

The first step is to register both the console app and the Web API application with Azure AD and fill in the configuration accordingly.

Web API

This is a step-by-step demonstration of registering the Web API with Azure AD.

1. Go to `https://portal.azure.com`.

2. Go to Azure Active Directory in the left navigation pane.

3. Click App Registrations.

4. Click New Registration.

5. Enter the name of your application, which can be changed later.

6. Enter **`https://localhost:44300`** as the redirect URL, and choose Web in the drop-down menu.

7. Click Register.

8. Copy the application ID. It is the client ID for your application and required for token validation.

9. Grant permissions to your application in API Permission and click the Grant Admin Consent button. Click Yes to confirm.

10. To find the tenant ID, go to App Registrations, click Endpoints, and fetch the tenant ID from any URL. A sample format is at `https://login.microsoftonline.com/{tenantId}/federationmetadata/2007-06/federationmetadata.xml`.

The tenant ID is always a valid GUID.

Console App

The following is a step-by-step demonstration of registering a console application with Azure AD.

1. Go to `https://portal.azure.com`.

2. Go to Azure Active Directory in the left navigation pane.

3. Click App Registrations.

4. Click New Registration.

5. Enter the name of your app.

6. Click Register.

7. Copy the application ID. It is the client ID for your application and required for token validation.

8. Go to API Permission ➤ Add a Permission. Select an API.

9. Search the newly added Web API and select the user impersonation permission.

10. Grant admin consent by clicking the Grant Admin Consent button.

11.   Generate a client secret. Go to Certificate and
      Secrets ➤ New Client Secret ➤ Give Description
      and Duration. Click Add. Copy the key and save it
      in a secured place. The key will not be visible again
      after you close the tile.

Now the configurations are ready. The next step is to create a
Windows console app and the Web API and enable Azure Active Directory
authentication for it.

Creating a Console App

After registering your application, follow these steps to create a console
application.

1.   Create a console application using the .NET
     Framework.

2.   Install the Microsoft.IdentityModel.Clients.
     ActiveDirectory package from NuGet (www.nuget.org).

3.   Add variables to configure the console app to get an
     access token, as follows.

```
private static string aadInstance = "https://login.
microsoftonline.com/{0}";
        private static string tenant = "tenant_id";
        private static string clientId = "client_id";
        private static string clientSecret = "client_
        secret";
    static string authority = String.Format(CultureInfo.
    InvariantCulture, aadInstance, tenant);
        private static string resourceId = "resource_id";
    private static string baseAddress = "api_Url";
```

4. Add a method that generates a token for the Web
    API, as follows.

```
authContext = new AuthenticationContext(authority);
        AuthenticationResult result = null;

        try
        {
            result = await authContext.AcquireToken
            Async(resourceId, clientId, redirect
            URI, new PlatformParameters(PromptBeha
            vior.Auto));
        }
        catch (Exception ex)
        {
            console.WriteLine("An error occurred.");
        }
```

A platform parameter takes input as a prompt
behavior. It has four values.

- **Auto**. Acquiring a token prompts the user for
  credentials only when necessary. If a token that
  meets the requirements is already cached, then the
  user is not prompted.

- **Always**. The user is prompted for credentials even if
  there is a token that meets the requirements already
  in the cache.

- **Never**. The user is not prompted for credentials.
  If prompting is necessary, then the AcquireToken
  request will fail.

- **Refresh**. Reauthorizes (through displaying a web view) the resource usage, making sure that the resulting access token contains updated claims. If user logon cookies are available, the user is not asked for credentials again, and the logon dialog dismisses automatically.

The next step calls the Web API to do the operation. Let's create the Web API, which is secured by Azure AD.

Creating a Web API

After creating a Windows console app, follow these steps to create a Web API.

1. Create a Web API MVC application using .NET Core 2.0.

2. Install the Microsoft.IdentityModel.Clients. ActiveDirectory package from NuGet (`www.nuget. org`).

3. Add the AzureAdOptions class to read the config, as shown in the following format.

```
public class AzureAdOptions
    {
public string ClientId { get; set; }
public string ClientSecret { get; set; }
public string Instance { get; set; }
public string Domain { get; set; }
public string TenantId { get; set; }
    }
```

4. Add configurations in appsettings.json in the
    following format. Fill in the configuration values as
    per the registration done in the previous step.

```
"AzureAd": {
    "Instance": "https://login.microsoftonline.com/",
    "Domain": "domain",
    "TenantId": "tenantId",
    "ClientId": "resourceId"
  }
```

5. Add the Extension method to configure the JWT
    options, as follows.

```
public static class AzureAdServiceCollection
Extensions
{
public static AuthenticationBuilder AddAzureAdBearer
(this AuthenticationBuilder builder)
=> builder.AddAzureAdBearer(_ => { });
public static AuthenticationBuilder AddAzure
AdBearer(this AuthenticationBuilder builder,
Action<AzureAdOptions> configureOptions)
{
builder.Services.Configure(configureOptions);
builder.Services.AddSingleton<IConfigureOptions
<JwtBearerOptions>, ConfigureAzureOptions>();
builder.AddJwtBearer();
return builder;
}
private class ConfigureAzureOptions: IConfigureNamed
Options<JwtBearerOptions>
```

```
{
private readonly AzureAdOptions _azureOptions;
public ConfigureAzureOptions(IOptions<AzureAdOptions>
azureOptions)
{
_azureOptions = azureOptions.Value;
}
public void Configure(string name, JwtBearerOptions
options)
{
options.Audience = _azureOptions.ClientId;
options.Authority = $"{_azureOptions.Instance}{_
azureOptions.TenantId}";
}
public void Configure(JwtBearerOptions options)
{
Configure(Options.DefaultName, options);
}
}
}
```

This code configures the JWT Bearer authentication
scheme. The client ID from AppSettings acts as the
audience. The AddJwtBearer method is provided by
Microsoft.AspNetCore.Authentication.Jwt Bearer.
This method automatically downloads the public
key based on the tenant ID provided, reads the
token in the header, and validates it using public
keys. If the validation is successful, then claims
obtained from the JWT token are added in the user
claims context; otherwise, a 401 error is returned.

6. Add the following code in startup.cs to read the
    configuration and call the Extension method to pass
    the configuration.

```
services.AddAuthentication(sharedOptions =>
{
        sharedOptions.DefaultScheme = JwtBearer
        Defaults.AuthenticationScheme;
})
.AddAzureAdBearer(options => Configuration.Bind
("AzureAd", options));
```

Your Web API is secured by Azure AD. Add a controller and expose a
Web API method.

If you face any difficulty in following these steps, please download the
code from the GitHub repository at

`https://github.com/aadfordevelopers/AadDemos/tree/master/`
`consoleAppAuthentication`.

To run the sample code, download it and add the configuration in the
code. Follow these steps to add the configuration.

1. Open the Web API's appsettings.json from the
    downloaded sample.

2. Add the tenant ID and client ID, which were
    obtained in the previous step.

3. Open the Windows console app's program.cs from
    the downloaded sample.

4. Add the tenant ID, resource ID, and client ID, which
    were obtained in the previous steps.

Now your sample is ready to run. Press F5. The Command prompt
screen is shown (see Figure 4-2). Make sure that both projects are marked
as startup projects.

Figure 4-2. *Console app command-line interface*

Press Enter. A call will go to the Microsoft Azure AD authorization endpoint, which will ask the user to log in using a web pop-up window, as shown in Figure 4-3.

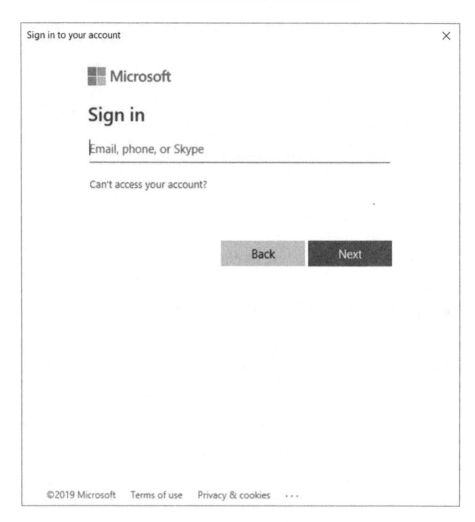

Figure 4-3. *Login screen in web pop-up window*

The user enters credentials and submits them. On successful validation of the credentials, Azure AD issues the authorization code. The authorization code in the console app requests an access token. After receiving an access token from AD, a request is sent to the Web API to fetch the data. The Web API validates the access token; on successful validation, data is returned and shown on the screen (see Figure 4-4).

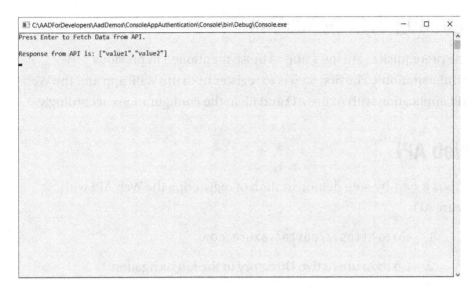

Figure 4-4. *Response from API*

Windows Presentation Foundation (WPF)

Windows Presentation Foundation (WPF) was launched in 2006 with .NET Framework 3.0. WPF is the upgraded name for Avalon. It is a graphical subsystem for Microsoft Windows to render UI. WPF uses an XAML (Extensible Application Markup Language)–based language to define and render the UI. In December 2018, Microsoft announced WPF as an open source project on GitHub.

WPF is widely used to develop desktop applications in the industry. Lots of companies have invested heavily in desktop applications in WPF. WPF applications are used in manufacturing, auditing, and finance.

To connect to the Web API from WPF, Microsoft Azure AD provides Azure AD authentication for WPF. Since WPF is a native Windows desktop app, the same protocol flow explained at the start of this chapter is used.

Running the Application

The prerequisites are the same as those mentioned in previous demonstrations. The first step is to register both the WPF app and the Web API application with Azure AD and fill in the configurations accordingly.

Web API

This is a step-by-step demonstration of registering the Web API with Azure AD.

1. Go to `https://portal.azure.com`.

2. Go to Azure Active Directory in the left navigation pane.

3. Click App Registrations.

4. Click New Registration.

5. Enter the name of your application, which can be changed later.

6. Enter `https://localhost:44300` as the redirect URL, and choose Web in the drop-down menu.

7. Click Register.

8. Copy the application ID. It is the client ID for your application and required for token validation.

9. Grant permissions to your application in API Permission and click the Grant Admin Consent button. Click Yes to confirm.

10.   To find the tenant ID, go to App Registrations,
      click Endpoints, and fetch the tenant
      ID from any URL. A sample format is at
      `https://login.microsoftonline.com/`
      `{tenantId}/federationmetadata/2007-06/`
      `federationmetadata.xml`.

The tenant ID is always a valid GUID.

WPF App

This is a step-by-step demonstration of registering a WPF application with
Azure AD.

1.   Go to `https://portal.azure.com`.

2.   Go to Azure Active Directory in the left
     navigation pane.

3.   Click App Registrations.

4.   Click New Registration.

5.   Enter the name of your app.

6.   Click Register.

7.   Copy the application ID. It is the client ID for your
     application and required for token validation.

8.   Go to API Permission ➤ Add a Permission. Select
     an API.

9.   Search the newly added Web API and select the user
     impersonation permission.

10. Grant admin consent by clicking the Grant Admin
     Consent button.

11. Generate a client secret. Go to Certificate and Secrets ➤ New Client Secret ➤ Give Description and Duration. Click Add. Copy the key and save it in a secured place. The key will not be visible again after you close the tile.

Now the configurations are ready. The next step is to create a WPF app and the Web API and enable Azure Active Directory authentication for it.

Creating a WPF App

After registering your application, follow these steps to create a WPF application.

1. Create a WPF application using the .NET Framework.

2. Install the Microsoft.IdentityModel.Clients. ActiveDirectory package from NuGet (www.nuget.org).

3. Add variables to configure the WPF app to get an access token, as follows.

```
private static string aadInstance = "https://login.
microsoftonline.com/{0}";
        private static string tenant = "tenant_id";
        private static string clientId = "client_id";
        private static string clientSecret = "client_
        secret";
    static string authority = String.Format(CultureInfo.
    InvariantCulture, aadInstance, tenant);
        private static string resourceId = "resource_
        id";
    private static string baseAddress = "api_Url";
```

4. Add a button and a textbox in MainWindow.xaml.cs.

5. Clicking the button fetches the access token from
    Azure AD. Use the following code.

```
private void Button_Click(object sender,
RoutedEventArgs e)
        {
            authContext = new AuthenticationContext
            (authority);
            txtData.Text = "Fetching Data......";
            GetData();
        }
```

GetData function internally will call the Azure AD to
fetch the access token.

```
AuthenticationResult result = null;

        try
        {
            result = await authContext.AcquireToken
            Async(resourceId, clientId, redirect
            URI, new PlatformParameters(Prompt
            Behavior.Auto));
        }
        catch (Exception ex)
        {
            txtData.Text = "An error occurred.";
        }
```

The platform parameters value is the same as it is in
the console app.

6. After fetching the access token, send an HTTP
    request to the Web API by adding an access token in
    the authorization header. This displays the result in
    the textbox.

Creating a Web API

After creating a WPF app, follow the same steps as previously shown to
create a Web API.

If you face any difficulty in following these steps, please download the
code from the GitHub repository at

`https://github.com/aadfordevelopers/AadDemos/tree/master/`
`WpfAuthentication.`

To run the sample code, download it and add the configuration in the
code. Follow these steps to add the configuration.

1. Open the Web API's appsettings.json from the
    downloaded sample.

2. Add the tenant ID and client ID, which were
    obtained in the previous step.

3. Open the WPF app's MainWindow.xaml.cs from the
    downloaded sample.

4. Add the tenant ID, resource ID, and client ID, which
    were obtained in previous steps.

Now your sample is ready to run. Press F5. The WPF Home screen is
shown (see Figure 4-5). Make sure that both projects are marked as startup
projects.

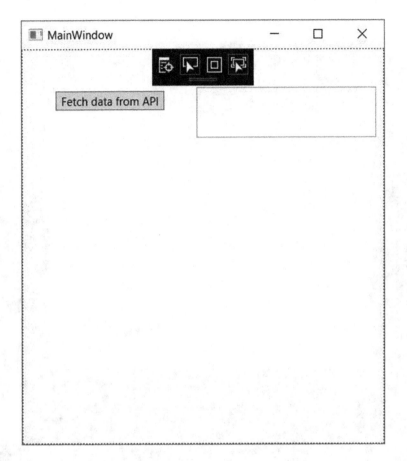

Figure 4-5. *WPF Home screen*

Click the "Fetch Data from API" button. The call goes to the Microsoft Azure AD authorization endpoint, which asks the user to log in using a web pop-up window, as shown in Figure 4-6.

Figure 4-6. *Login screen in web pop-up window*

The user enters the credentials and submits them. On successful validation of the credentials, Azure AD issues the authorization code. The authorization code in the WPF app requests an access token. After receiving the access token from AD, the request is sent to the Web API to fetch the data. The Web API validates the access token, and on successful validation, the data is returned and shown on screen (see Figure 4-7).

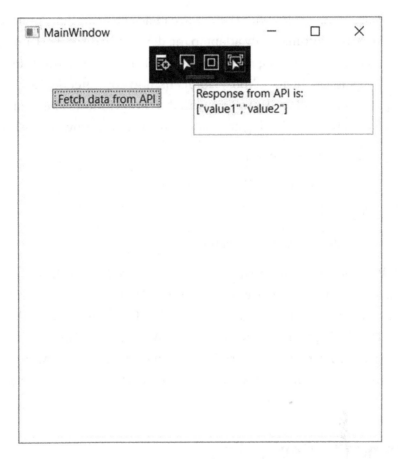

Figure 4-7. *Data from API*

Universal Windows Platform (UWP)

There are different types of devices running on Windows 10, such as mobile devices, tablets, surface devices, laptops, TVs, and so forth. Designing an app for each device again and again would take a lot of development effort. To solve this problem, Microsoft came up with Universal Windows Platform (UWP) applications, which are designed to run on any device using the Windows 10 OS.

UWP also uses XAML. With UWP, you can design beautifully polished applications that automatically adapt to the device on which it is running.

With UWP, you can design applications for IoT devices, mobile devices, PCs, tablets, surface devices, Xbox, HoloLens, and any other device running on Windows 10. UWP aligns with the One Windows Platform Microsoft policy. The following are some of the features provided by UWP.

- Adaptive user interface

- Natural user input based on the device

- One SDK

- One store and one dev center

UWP applications can be written in many different languages, including C#, C++, Visual Basic, and JavaScript. In this chapter, we will develop a small UWP app based on C# and XAML, which will fetch data from an HTTP triggered function secured by Azure Active Directory. We are using an HTTP triggered Azure function instead of the Web API; a UWP application cannot communicate with a localhost API due to enhanced security.

Running the Application

To develop a Universal Windows Platform application using Azure Active Directory authentication, you need the following software and completed prerequisites.

- Visual Studio 2017 (If you don't have a license, you can use the Community edition.)

- .NET Core 2.1 SDK

- UWP SDK (This is installed using a Visual Studio installer. Open the Visual Studio 2017 installer from the Start menu by typing "Visual Studio Installer" or by opening Visual Studio and going to Tools ➤ Get Tools and Features. Look for UWP and install all the SDKs related to UWP.)

- an Azure subscription and an Azure AD tenant

- a user account in your Azure AD tenant

The first step is to register both the UWP app and Azure AD Function application with Azure AD and fill in the configurations accordingly.

HTTP Triggered Azure Function Endpoint

The following is a step-by-step demonstration of registering an HTTP triggered Azure Function app with Azure AD.

1. Go to `https://portal.azure.com`.

2. Go to Azure Active Directory in the left navigation pane.

3. Click App Registrations.

4. Click New Registration.

5. Enter the name of your application, which can be changed later.

6. Enter **https://localhost:44364** as the redirect URL, and choose Web in the drop-down menu.

7. Click Register.

8. Copy the application ID. It is the client ID for your application and required for token validation.

133

9.   Grant permissions to your application in API Permission and click the Grant Admin Consent button. Click Yes to confirm.

10. To find the tenant ID, go to App Registrations, click Endpoints, and fetch the tenant ID from any URL. A sample format is at `https://login.microsoftonline.com/` `{tenantId}/federationmetadata/2007-06/` `federationmetadata.xml`.

The tenant ID is always a valid GUID.

UWP App

The following is a step-by-step demonstration of registering a UWP application with Azure AD.

1.   Go to `https://portal.azure.com`.

2.   Go to Azure Active Directory in the left navigation pane.

3.   Click App Registrations.

4.   Click New Registration.

5.   Enter the name of your app.

6.   Click Register.

7.   Copy the application ID. It is the client ID for your application and required for token validation.

8.   Go to API Permission ➤ Add a Permission. Select an API.

9.   Search the newly added HTTP triggered Azure function app and select the user impersonation permission.

10. Grant admin consent by clicking the Grant Admin Consent button.

11. Generate a client secret. Go to Certificate and Secrets ➤ New Client Secret ➤ Give Description and Duration. Click Add. Copy the key and save it in a secured place. The key will not be visible again after you close the tile.

Now the configurations are ready. The next step is to create a UWP app and an HTTP triggered Azure function and enable Azure Active Directory authentication for it.

Creating a UWP App

After registering your application, follow these steps to create a UWP application.

1. Create a UWP application using the .NET Framework.

2. Install the Microsoft.IdentityModel.Clients.Active Directory package from NuGet (www.nuget.org).

3. Add variables to configure the UWP app to get an access token, as follows.

```
private static string aadInstance = "https://login.
microsoftonline.com/{0}";
        private static string tenant = "tenant_id";
        private static string clientId = "client_id";
        private static string clientSecret = "client_
        secret";
    static string authority = String.Format(CultureInfo.
    InvariantCulture, aadInstance, tenant);
```

```
            private static string resourceId = "resource_id";
        private static string baseAddress = "api_Url";
        private Uri redirectURI = null;
```

4. Fetch the redirect URI value using the following
   code in the constructor.

```
redirectURI = Windows.Security.Authentication.
Web.WebAuthenticationBroker.GetCurrentApplication
CallbackUri();
```

5. While running the application, add a breakpoint
   on the preceding line, note the redirect URI, and
   update the same in the Azure portal. This is because
   a reply URI or redirect URI is generated at run
   time; the same should be updated in the Azure app
   registration.

6. Add a button and textbox in MainWindow.xaml.cs.

7. Clicking the button fetches the access token from
   Azure AD. Use the following code.

```
private void Button_Click(object sender, Routed
EventArgs e)
        {
                GetData();
        }
```

GetData is an async function that internally calls
Azure AD to fetch the access token.

```
AuthenticationResult result = null;

        try
        {
```

```
        result = await authContext.AcquireToken
        Async(resourceId, clientId,
        redirectURI, new PlatformParameters
        (PromptBehavior.Auto));
    }
    catch (Exception ex)
    {
        txtData.Text = "An error occurred.";
    }
```

The platform parameters value is the same as the one in the console app.

8. After fetching an access token, send the HTTP request to the Web API by adding an access token in the authorization header. This displays the result in the textbox.

Creating an HTTP Triggered Azure Function

The next step is to create and configure an HTTP triggered Azure function endpoint.

1. Go to http://portal.azure.com.

2. Create a function app with default options. Make sure the runtime stack is .NET.

3. In the Azure function app, add an HTTP trigger Azure function.

4. Use the default C# code that is already there; only change the object result to $"Hello, {name}. This is a response from the Azure function."

5. Note the Azure AD function app URL by clicking the "Get function" link.

6. Click Integrate and select Anonymous as the authorization level, as shown in Figure 4-8.

Figure 4-8. *Authorization screen for HTTP triggered Azure function*

7. Go to Function app ➤ Platform Features, and then Select Authentication/Authorization.

8. Enable app service authentication.

9. Choose Azure Active Directory as the authentication provider (see Figure 4-9).

Authentication / Authorization

🔖 Save   ✖ Discard

Authentication / Authorization

ℹ️ To enable Authentication / Authorization, please ensure all your custom domains have correspor

App Service Authentication

| Off | **On** |

Action to take when request is not authenticated

Log in with Azure Active Directory

Authentication Providers

◈ Azure Active Directory
Configured (Advanced)

◼ Facebook
Not Configured

◼ Google
Not Configured

◼ Twitter
Not Configured

◼ Microsoft
Not Configured

Advanced Settings

Token Store | Off | **On** |

Figure 4-9. *Authentication/Authorization for Azure Function*

10. Add the client ID, which you generated in the previous step when registering the Azure function app with Azure AD.

11. Add the issuer URL as `https://login.windows.net/{tenantId}`.

139

12. In the "Action to take when the request is not
     authenticated" drop-down menu, select "Log in
     with Azure Active Directory".

13. Click Save (see Figure 4-10).

 Azure Active Directory Settings   □ ✕

Active Directory Authentication

These settings allow users to sign in with Azure Active Directory. Click here to learn
more. Learn more

Management mode ❶ | Off | Express | **Advanced** |

Client ID

b68f72a1-f591-4512-b22b-03718b8eea41

Issuer Url ❶

https://login.windows.net/35d622d5-3f93-42b1-8984-3e2606dbe321

Client Secret (Optional)

ALLOWED TOKEN AUDIENCES

                                                                        ...

Figure 4-10. *Azure Active Directory authentication configuration for*
Azure Function

If you face any difficulty in following these steps, please download the
code from GitHub at `https://github.com/mohit797/AadDemos/tree/`
`master/UWPAuthentication`.

Before opening the solution, make sure that you have installed the
latest version of Visual Studio 2019 SDKs for UWP.

To run the sample code, download it and follow these steps to add the configuration.

1. Open MainPage.xaml.cs from the downloaded sample.

2. Add the tenant ID, resource ID, and client ID, which were obtained in previous steps.

Now your sample is ready to run. Press F5. The UWP app screen is shown in Figure 4-11.

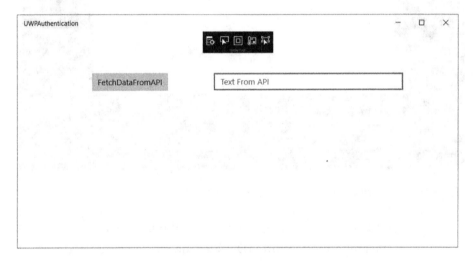

Figure 4-11. *UWP Home screen*

Click the "Fetch Data from API" button. The call goes to the Microsoft Azure AD authorization endpoint, which asks the user to log in using a web pop-up window, as shown in Figure 4-12.

Figure 4-12. *Login using web pop-up window*

The user enters the credentials and submits them. On successful validation of the credentials, Azure AD issues the authorization code. The authorization code in the UWP app requests an access token. After receiving the access token from AD, the request is sent to the HTTP triggered Azure function to fetch the data. The Azure function validates the access token. On successful validation, the data is returned and shown on the screen (see Figure 4-13).

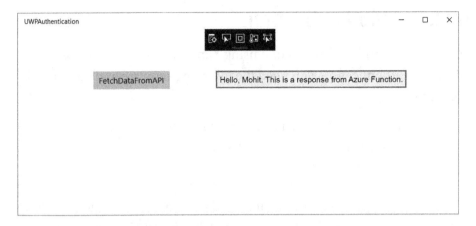

Figure 4-13.   Data from HTTP triggered Azure function

Android Application

Android is one of the most popular and most used mobile and tablet operating systems in the world. A lot of applications are developed in Android on a daily basis. Windows and iOS are two other operating systems that are equally popular.

Developing the same application for these three operating systems consumes a lot of human effort if developed separately. Microsoft came up with a platform that can deliver native apps for Android, iOS, and Windows by using a single .NET code base called Xamarin.

Applications using Xamarin can be developed on Windows or Mac. Apps developed with Xamarin offer the following features.

- Native UI

- Native API access

- Native performance

Next, we discuss how Android apps are authenticated using Xamarin and Microsoft Azure Active Directory. Android fetches the data from an HTTP triggered Azure function secured by Azure AD.

143

Running the Application

To develop an Android application using Xamarin and Azure Active Directory authentication, you need the following software and completed prerequisites.

- Visual Studio 2017 (If you don't have a license, you can use the Community edition).

- .NET Core 2.1 SDK

- Xamarin SDK (It can be installed using a Visual Studio installer. You can open the Visual Studio 2017 installer either from the Start menu by typing "Visual Studio Installer" or by opening Visual Studio and then Tools ➤ Get Tools and Features. Look for Xamarin and install all the SDKs related to Android development.)

- an Azure Subscription and an Azure AD tenant

- a user account in your Azure AD tenant

The first step is to register both the Android app and the Azure AD Function application with Azure AD and fill in the configurations accordingly.

HTTP Triggered Azure Function Endpoint

The following is a step-by-step demonstration of registering an HTTP triggered Azure Function app with Azure AD.

1. Go to `https://portal.azure.com`.

2. Go to Azure Active Directory in the left navigation pane.

3. Click App Registrations.

4. Click New Registration.

5. Enter the name of your application, which can be changed later.

6. Enter **https://localhost:44364** as the redirect URL, and choose Web in the drop-down menu.

7. Click Register.

8. Copy the application ID. It is the client ID for your application and required for token validation.

9. Grant permissions to your application in API Permission and click the Grant Admin Consent button. Click Yes to confirm.

10. To find the tenant ID, go to App Registrations, click Endpoints, and fetch the tenant ID from any URL. A sample format is at https://login.microsoftonline.com/ {tenantId}/federationmetadata/2007-06/ federationmetadata.xml.

The tenant ID is always a valid GUID.

Android App

The following is a step-by-step demonstration of registering an Android application with Azure AD.

1. Go to https://portal.azure.com.

2. Go to Azure Active Directory in the left navigation pane.

3. Click App Registrations.

4. Click New Registration.

5.   Enter the name of your app.

6.   Click Register.

7.   Copy the application ID. It is the client ID for your application and required for token validation.

8.   Go to API Permission ➤ Add a Permission. Select an API.

9.   Search the newly added HTTP triggered Azure function app and select the user impersonation permission.

10. Grant admin consent by clicking the Grant Admin Consent button.

11. Generate a client secret. Go to Certificate and Secrets ➤ New Client Secret ➤ Give Description and Duration. Click Add. Copy the key and save it in a secured place. The key will not be visible again after you close the tile.

Now the configurations are ready. The next step is to create an Android app and an HTTP triggered Azure function and enable Azure Active Directory authentication for it.

Creating an Android App

After registering your application, follow these steps to create an Android application.

1.   Create an Android application using the .NET Framework.

2.   Add a .NET Standard Class Library project and install the Microsoft.IdentityModel.Clients.ActiveDirectory package from NuGet (www.nuget.org).

3. Refer to the project in Android Project.

4. Add a static class in the Class library project.

5. Add variables in the static class to configure the
    Android app to get an access token, as follows.

```
const string clientId = "clientId";
const string authority = "https://login.microsoft
online.com/common/";
const string resourceId = "resourceId";
const string baseAddress = "https://azurefunctionauth.
azurewebsites.net/api/HttpTrigger1";
static Uri redirectURI = new Uri("https://login.
microsoftonline.com/common/oauth2/nativeclient");
```

6. Add a method in the static class, which accepts
    platform parameters as input and gets the access
    token from Azure AD. Use the following code.

```
AuthenticationContext authContext = new Authentication
Context(authority);
AuthenticationResult result = await authContext.
AcquireTokenAsync(resourceId, clientId, redirectURI,
platformParameters);
```

7. The platform parameters value is the same as the
    one in the console app.

8. Add a button and a textbox in the Android app.
    In the Activity class, clicking the button fetches
    the access token by passing platform parameters
    like "new PlatformParameters(this)". this
    refers to the Activity class, which inherits from
    AppCompatActivity.

9. To receive the authentication callback after entering the username and password, the following code is required in the Activity class. It sets the authentication response from the web view for an acquisition token.

```
protected override void OnActivityResult(int
requestCode, Result resultCode, Intent data)
        {
            base.OnActivityResult(requestCode,
            resultCode, data);
            AuthenticationAgentContinuationHelper.
            SetAuthenticationAgentContinuationEvent
            Args(requestCode, resultCode, data);
        }
```

Creating an HTTP Triggered Azure Function

The next step is to create an HTTP triggered Azure function endpoint. Follow the same steps to create an HTTP triggered Azure function that were used for developing an UWP application.

If you face any difficulty in following these steps, please download the code from the GitHub repository at https://github.com/ aadfordevelopers/AadDemos/tree/master/AndroidAuthentication.

Before opening the solution, make sure that you have installed the latest version of the Visual Studio 2019 SDKs for the Xamarin Android platform.

To run the sample code, download it and follow these steps to add the configuration.

1. Open FetchDataFromAPI.cs from the downloaded sample.

2. Add the tenant ID, resource ID, and client ID, which were obtained in previous steps.

Now your sample is ready to run. To run the sample, connect your Android mobile device to your laptop using a USB cable. The mobile device needs to be running (at a minimum) version 8.1 (Oreo) with developer options on. Or, set up an Android emulator with version 8.1 (Oreo).

Note   Setting up an Android emulator or an installing emulator is not within the scope of this book. Please refer to `https://docs.microsoft.com/en-us/xamarin/android/` for further help.

To demo this solution, we have installed the app on a mobile device running version 9.0. When users open the app in Android, they see the screen shown in Figure 4-14.

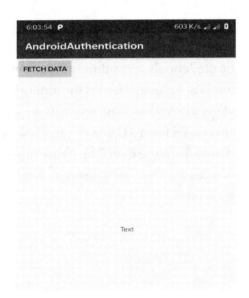

Figure 4-14. *Android app Home screen*

Click the Fetch Data button. The call goes to the Microsoft Azure AD authorization endpoint, which redirects the user to the Login page, as shown in Figure 4-15.

Figure 4-15. *Login screen inside Android application*

The user enters the credentials and submits them. On successful validation of the credentials, Azure AD issues the authorization code. The authorization code in the Android app requests an access token. After receiving an access token from AD, the request is sent to the HTTP triggered Azure function to fetch the data. The Azure function validates the access token, and on successful validation, the data is returned and shown on the screen (see Figure 4-16).

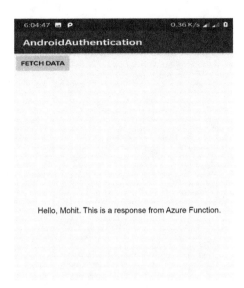

Figure 4-16. *Data from HTTP triggered Azure function*

Summary

This chapter showed you how to enable user-based Azure AD authentication for native applications. All native applications follow an authorization code grant flow in an OAuth 2.0 specification. We started with a console application and WPF application. We moved on to Universal Windows Platform for all Windows devices, and then to Android authentication using Xamarin, which can be extended to iOS and Windows applications as well.

In the next chapter, we discuss authentication for daemon applications (applications authenticating without any user interaction).

CHAPTER 5

Daemon Application Authentication

In the previous chapters, we discussed various, user-based, authentication scenarios for different web applications and native applications. In this chapter, we focus on daemon application authentication. A daemon application is a background process or application that runs without user interaction.

Azure WebJobs, Azure Functions, background processes, and so forth, are applications that run without direct user interaction. To secure the communication of these background applications with other Web APIs, a client credential flow from OAuth 2.0 (explained in Chapter 2) can be used with Microsoft Azure AD. In this chapter, we cover daemon authentication using the following methods.

- Client credential authentication

- Certificate-based client credential authentication

Client Credential Authentication Flow

A client credential authentication flow is used when there is a need for running a background or headless job, or for running a process in the application's identity instead of the user's identity. The following are some examples of where client credential authentication flow is needed.

© Manas Mayank and Mohit Garg 2019
M. Mayank and M. Garg, *Developing Applications with Azure Active Directory*,
https://doi.org/10.1007/978-1-4842-5040-2_5

- Azure Functions

- Azure WebJobs

- Integration tests

- A web app communicating with the Web API in an application's context (to get user-independent data and application-dependent data).

Figure 5-1 is a diagram showing the sequence of events that happen when authenticating daemon applications using Azure Active Directory.

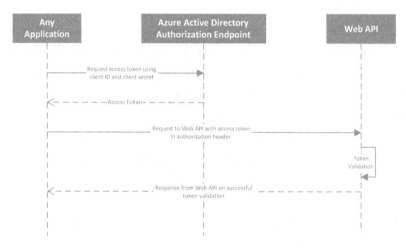

Figure 5-1. *Sequence diagram for daemon application authentication*

The following sequence of events are performed during authentication.

1. As soon as the background process starts, the request is sent to Azure AD with the client ID and client secret to get the access token.

2. The request with the access token in the authorization header is sent to the Web API.

3. The Web API is secured by Azure Active Directory authentication, which validates the token.

4. On successful validation, the response is returned to call the application.

Running Your Application

To develop a Windows console application using Azure Active Directory daemon authentication, you need the following software and completed prerequisites.

- Visual Studio 2017 (If you don't have a license, you can use the Community edition for learning.)

- .NET Core 2.1 SDK

- an Azure subscription and Azure AD tenant

- a user account in your Azure AD tenant

To run the application and do the authentication using client credential flow, you need to register both the console app and the Web API application with Azure AD. The next section is a step-by-step demonstration of registering your applications with Azure AD.

Web API

The following is a step-by-step demonstration of registering the Web API with Azure AD.

1. Go to https://portal.azure.com.

2. Go to Azure Active Directory in the left navigation pane.

3. Click App Registrations.

4. Click New Registration.

5. Enter the name for your application, which can be changed later.

6. Enter **https://localhost:44300** as the redirect URL, and choose Web from the drop-down menu.

7. Click Register.

8. Copy the application ID. It is the client ID for your application and required for token validation.

9. Grant permissions to your application in API Permission. Click the Grant Admin Consent button. Click Yes to confirm.

10. To find the tenant ID, go to App Registrations, click Endpoints, and fetch the tenant ID from any URL. A sample format is at https://login.microsoftonline.com/ {tenantId}/federationmetadata/2007-06/ federationmetadata.xml.

Tenant ID is always a valid GUID.

Console App

Please follow these steps to register a console app with Azure AD.

1. Go to https://portal.azure.com.

2. Go to Azure Active Directory in the left navigation pane.

3. Click App Registrations.

4. Click New Registration.

5.   Enter the name of your app.

6.   Click Register.

7.   Copy the application ID. It is the client ID for your application and required for token validation.

8.   For client credential flow, the user impersonation permission is not required because there is no user involved.

9.   Generate the client secret. Go to Certificate and Secrets ➤ New Client Secret ➤ Give Description and Duration and click Add.

10.   Copy the key and save it in a secure place. This key will not be visible again after you close the tile.

The configurations are ready. The next step is to create the Windows console app and Web API and enable Azure Active Directory authentication for it.

Creating a Console App

After registering your application, follow these steps to create a console application.

1.   Create a console application using .NET Framework.

2.   Install the Microsoft.IdentityModel.Clients. ActiveDirectory package from NuGet (www.nuget.org).

3.   Add variables to configure the console app to get the access token, as shown next.

```
private static string aadInstance = "https://login.
microsoftonline.com/{0}";
        private static string tenant = "tenant_id";
```

```
private static string clientId = "client_id";
private static string clientSecret = "client_
secret";
static string authority = String.Format(CultureInfo.
InvariantCulture, aadInstance, tenant);
private static string resourceId =
"resource_id";
private static string baseAddress = "api_Url";
```

4. Add a method that will generate a token for the Web
   API, as shown next.

```
authContext = new AuthenticationContext(authority);
AuthenticationResult result = null;

try
{
    ClientCredential clientCredential =
    new ClientCredential(clientId,
    clientSecret);
        var authResult = autheContext.
        AcquireTokenAsync(resourceId,
        clientCredential).Result;
}
catch (Exception ex)
{
    Console.WriteLine("An error occurred.");
}
```

The next step is to call a Web API to do the operation. Let's create a
Web API that is secured by Azure AD.

Creating a Web API

After creating the Windows console app, follow these steps to create
a Web API.

1. Create a Web API MVC application using .NET Core
   2.0.

2. Install the Microsoft.IdentityModel.Clients.Active
   Directory package from NuGet (www.nuget.org).

3. Add the AzureAdOptions class to read the config, as
   shown in the following format.

   ```
   public class AzureAdOptions
       {
   public string ClientId { get; set; }
   public string ClientSecret { get; set; }
   public string Instance { get; set; }
   public string Domain { get; set; }
   public string TenantId { get; set; }
       }
   ```

4. Add the configuration in appsettings.json in the
   following format. Fill the configuration values as per
   the registration done in the previous step.

   ```
   "AzureAd": {
       "Instance": "https://login.microsoftonline.com/",
       "Domain": "domain",
       "TenantId": "tenantId",
       "ClientId": "resourceId"
     }
   ```

5. Add the Extension method to configure the JWT
    options, as shown next.

```
public static class AzureAdServiceCollection
Extensions
{
public static AuthenticationBuilder
AddAzureAdBearer(this AuthenticationBuilder builder)
=> builder.AddAzureAdBearer(_ => { });
public static AuthenticationBuilder
AddAzureAdBearer(this AuthenticationBuilder builder,
Action<AzureAdOptions> configureOptions)
{
builder.Services.Configure(configureOptions);
builder.Services.AddSingleton<IConfigureOptions
<JwtBearerOptions>, ConfigureAzureOptions>();
builder.AddJwtBearer();
return builder;
}
private class ConfigureAzureOptions: IConfigureNamed
Options<JwtBearerOptions>
{
private readonly AzureAdOptions _azureOptions;
public ConfigureAzureOptions(IOptions<AzureAdOptions>
azureOptions)
{
_azureOptions = azureOptions.Value;
}
public void Configure(string name, JwtBearerOptions
options)
```

```
{
options.Audience = _azureOptions.ClientId;
options.Authority = $"{_azureOptions.Instance}{_
azureOptions.TenantId}";
}
public void Configure(JwtBearerOptions options)
{
Configure(Options.DefaultName, options);
}
}
}
```

This code configures the JWT bearer authentication scheme. The client ID from appsettings.json acts as the audience.

The AddJwtBearer method is provided by Microsoft.AspNetCore. Authentication.JwtBearer. This method automatically downloads the public key based on the tenant ID.

Read the token from the header and validate it using public keys. If the validation is successful, then claims obtained from the JWT token will be added in the user claims context; otherwise, a 401 error will be returned.

6. Add the following code to startup.cs to read the configuration and call the extension method to pass the configuration.

```
services.AddAuthentication(sharedOptions =>
{
        sharedOptions.DefaultScheme =
JwtBearerDefaults.AuthenticationScheme;
})
.AddAzureAdBearer(options => Configuration.
Bind("AzureAd", options));
```

Your Web API is secured by Azure AD. Add a controller and expose a Web API method.

If you face any difficulties in following these steps, please download the code from the GitHub repository at `https://github.com/aadfordevelopers/AadDemos/tree/master/ClientCredential`.

To run the sample code, download it as directed and add the configuration. Follow these steps to add the configuration.

1. Open appsettings.json in the Web API from the downloaded sample.

2. Add the tenant ID and the client ID obtained in the previous step.

3. Open program.cs from the Windows console app in the downloaded sample.

4. Add the tenant ID, resource ID, and client ID obtained in the previous steps.

Now your sample is ready to run. Press F5. The Command Prompt screen appears, as shown in Figure 5-2. Make sure that both projects are marked as a startup project.

Figure 5-2. *Console app command-line interface*

Press Enter. The call goes to the Microsoft Azure AD authorization endpoint using a client credential flow. On the successful validation of the credentials, Azure AD will issue an access token. After receiving the access token from AD, a request is sent to the Web API to fetch the data. The Web API validates the access token; on successful validation, the data is returned, as shown in Figure 5-3.

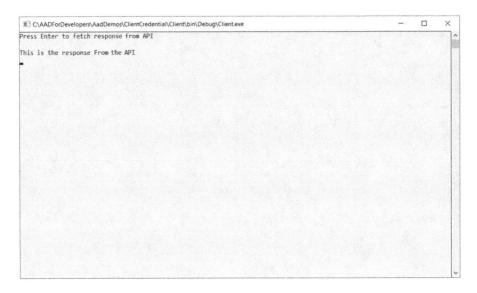

Figure 5-3. *Response from API*

Even though the client credential flow is totally secure, if a secret is leaked, the APIs could be easily compromised without anyone knowing. The user will not discover this until after the damage is done. Instead of using a client secret in the client credential flow, a better approach is to use certificates. Certificates can be installed on a local machine or reside in an Azure key vault.

Client Credential Authentication Flow Using a Certificate

In certificate-based client credential flow, the certificate acts as a client secret. During the authentication process, it reads the certificate from the local machine and passes the certificate to Azure AD to receive the access token. Certificates are linked to the Azure AD app.

The diagram in Figure 5-4 shows the sequence of events that happen when performing certificate-based client credential authentication for daemon applications using Azure Active Directory.

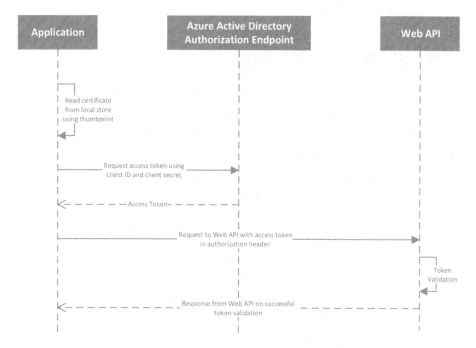

Figure 5-4. *Sequence diagram for client credential app authentication using certificates*

The following sequence of events are performed during authentication.

1. The background process tries to find the certificate from the local store by using a thumbprint.

2. The request is sent to Azure AD with the client ID and certificate to get an access token.

3. The request for an access token in the authorization header is sent to the Web API.

165

4.   The Web API secured by Azure Active Directory authentication validates the token.

5.   On successful validation, a response is returned to call the application.

Running Your Application

To run the application and authenticate using a client credential flow, you need to register both the console app and the Web API application with Azure AD. Also, you need to generate a certificate and link it to the Azure AD client app by using a manifest.

Here is a step-by-step demonstration of generating a certificate and registering your applications with Azure.

1.   Open Windows PowerShell from the Start menu.

2.   Execute the following PowerShell command:
```
"$cert=New-SelfSignedCertificate -Subject
"CN=CertificateClient" -CertStoreLocation
"Cert:\CurrentUser\My" -KeyExportPolicy
Exportable -KeySpec Signature"
```
The command creates a self-signed certificate in your local computer under the current user. The certificate key is exportable. Certificate keys are exported and added in the Azure app manifest.

3.   Execute the following commands to export the keys from the certificate in the same PowerShell window.

- `$cerRawData = $cert.RawData`

- `$value = [System.Convert]::ToBase64String($cerRawData)`

- `$hash = $cert.GetCertHash()`

- `$base64Thumbprint = [System.Convert]::ToBase64String($hash)`

- `$keyid = [System.Guid]::NewGuid().ToString()`

- `$jsonObj = @{customKeyIdentifier=$base64Thumbprint;keyId=$keyid;type="AsymmetricX509Cert";usage="Verify";value=$value}`

- `$certificateKeys=ConvertTo-Json @($jsonObj) | Out-File "certificateKeys.txt"`

The certificate keys are saved on your local machine; they are in JSON format.

Now you need to upload these keys in the client app manifest. The steps in the next section create the app and upload the keys in the manifest. Before that, the API Azure AD application should be there.

Web API

Here is the step-by-step demonstration of registering the Web API with Azure AD.

1. Go to `https://portal.azure.com`.

2. Go to Azure Active Directory in the left navigation pane.

3. Click App Registrations.

4. Click New Registration.

5. Enter the name of your application, which can be changed later.

6. Enter **`https://localhost:44300`** as the redirect URL, and choose Web from the drop-down menu.

7. Click Register.

8. Copy the application ID. It is the client ID for your application and required for token validation.

9. Grant permissions to your application in API Permission. Click the Grant Admin Consent button. Click Yes to confirm.

10. To find the tenant ID, go to App Registrations, click Endpoints, and fetch the tenant ID from any URL. The sample format is at `https://login.microsoftonline.com/ {tenantId}/federationmetadata/2007-06/ federationmetadata.xml`.

The tenant ID is always a valid GUID.

Console App

The following is a step-by-step demonstration of registering a console application with Azure AD.

1. Go to `https://portal.azure.com`.

2. Go to Azure Active Directory in the left navigation pane.

3. Click App Registrations.

4. Click New App Registration.

5. Enter the name of your native app.

6. Click Register.

7. Copy the application ID. It is the client ID for your application and required for token validation.

8. For a client credential flow using certificates, user impersonation permission is not required because there is no user involved.

9. Now upload the keys generated in the previous step in the manifest. Go to Manifest ➤ Edit.

10. An editor opens. Find the keyCredentials JSON element. The value of this element should be empty, like this [ ].

11. Copy and paste the certificate keys (obtained in the previous step) to replace the square brackets.

12. Click Save.

After registering the console app with Azure Active Directory, you need to add the configuration to the code. Follow these steps to add the configuration.

1. Open program.cs from the downloaded sample.

2. Add the tenant ID, resource ID, client ID, and the certificate name, which was obtained in previous steps.

Now your sample is ready to run. It will have the same output shown in the previous flow.

Creating a Console App

After registering your application, follow these steps to create a console application.

1. Create a console application using the .NET Framework.

2. Install the Microsoft.IdentityModel.Clients.Active Directory package from NuGet (www.nuget.org).

3. Add variables to configure the console app to get an access token, as shown next.

```
private static string aadInstance = "https://login.
microsoftonline.com/{0}";
        private static string tenant = "tenant_id";
        private static string clientId = "client_id";
private static string certName = "certName";
static string authority = String.Format(CultureInfo.
InvariantCulture, aadInstance, tenant);
        private static string resourceId = "resource_id";
 private static string baseAddress = "api_Url";
```

4. Add a method that will read a certificate from the local store, as shown next.

```
private static X509Certificate2 ReadCertificate
FromStore(string certName)
{
    X509Certificate2 cert = null;
    X509Store store = new X509Store(StoreName.My,
    StoreLocation.CurrentUser);
    store.Open(OpenFlags.ReadOnly);
    X509Certificate2Collection certCollection = store.
    Certificates;

    // Find unexpired certificates.
    X509Certificate2Collection currentCerts =
    certCollection.Find(X509FindType.FindByTimeValid,
    DateTime.Now, false);

    // From the collection of unexpired certificates,
        find the ones with the correct name.
```

```
X509Certificate2Collection signingCert = current
Certs.Find(X509FindType.FindBySubjectDistinguished
Name, certName, false);

// Return the first certificate in the collection,
    has the right name and is current.
cert = signingCert.OfType<X509Certificate2>().
OrderByDescending(c => c.NotBefore).
FirstOrDefault();
store.Close();
return cert;
}
```

This function takes the certificate name as
input and returns it in X509Certificate2 format.
The certificate name should be passed in the
CN={CertificateName} format. The following is a
step-by-step explanation.

a. Create an instance of X509Store for the current user to locate
   all the certificates in the local store in read-only mode.

b. Populate all the valid certificates in a variable.

c. Iterate all the valid certificates and find the desired certificate
   by certificate name.

5. Add a method that generates a token for the Web
   API by using a certificate, as shown next.

```
authContext = new AuthenticationContext(authority);
            AuthenticationResult result = null;
X509Certificate2 cert = ReadCertificateFromStore
(certName);

        try
        {
```

```
            ClientCredential clientCredential = new
            ClientCredential(clientId, cert);
            var authResult = autheContext.AcquireToken
            Async(resourceId, clientCredential).Result;
    }
    catch (Exception ex)
    {
            Console.WriteLine("An error occurred.");
    }
```

The next step is to call the Web API to do the operation. Let's create a Web API that is secured by Azure AD.

Creating a Web API

After creating the Windows console app, follow the same steps to create a .NET Core Web API secured by Azure AD, as done in the client credentials flow.

If you face any difficulties in following these steps, please download the code from the GitHub repository at https://github.com/aadfordevelopers/AadDemos/tree/master/CertificateClient.

To run the sample code, download it as directed. Configure the console application and the Web API.

To configure the console application, follow these steps.

1. Open program.cs from the downloaded sample.

2. Add the tenant ID, resource ID, client ID, and the certificate name, which you obtained in previous steps.

To configure the Web API, follow these steps.

1. Open appsettings.json from the downloaded sample.

2. Add the tenant ID and client ID, which were obtained in previous step.

Now your sample is ready to run. The output of this sample is the same as the client credential flow, but instead of generating a token using a client and secret, a token is generated using a client and certificate.

Summary

In this chapter, you learned how to call Web APIs secured by Azure Active Directory from background or daemon applications using a client credential flow. You also learned client credential flow using a certificate instead of a client secret.

Chapter 6 focuses on custom data extensions using Microsoft Graph.

CHAPTER 6

Active Directory Custom Data Extensions

In previous chapters, we discussed various user-based and application-based authentication scenarios for different web applications and native applications. This chapter focuses on custom data extensions.

Custom Data Extensions

By default, Azure AD provides some predefined properties for resources such as the user, group, organization, and so forth. These predefined properties include name, description, ID, phone number, and so forth. But, these properties may not be enough for some business needs, and you may want to add custom properties. For example, you may want to add users' hobbies to the user resource. This custom data can be extended to resources by using custom data extensions.

© Manas Mayank and Mohit Garg 2019
M. Mayank and M. Garg, *Developing Applications with Azure Active Directory*,
https://doi.org/10.1007/978-1-4842-5040-2_6

Microsoft Graph with Azure AD

Microsoft Graph is a gateway that provides various APIs to access Azure Active Directory resources and Office 365 resources. In the context of this chapter, we will use the Microsoft Graph API for Azure AD to access various resources (user, group, etc.) and extend them.

There are two types of extensions offered by Microsoft Graph.

- **Open extensions**. Allows you to add untyped data directly to the resource instance.

- **Schema extension**. Allows you to define a schema on the resource; by using a schema, you can extend the resource instance.

With the help of the Microsoft Graph API, custom data can be extended on the resource instance. To authenticate the Microsoft Graph API, Azure AD supports the following OAuth 2.0 authentication flows.

- **Code grant flow**. This flow authentication is done in the context of the user.

- **Client credential flow**. This flow authentication is done using a client credential flow. You can use either a client ID and a client secret, or a client ID and a certificate to generate an access token for the Graph API.

Both flows have pros and cons. Based on your business needs, you can decide which flow should be used; for example,

- If the number of users is low and no one else is able to read or update the data using Microsoft Graph, then you should use a code grant flow.

- If you want to open your application to all users to read and to update the data using Microsoft Graph, then you should use a client credential flow.

In both flows, the Azure AD app should delegate access to Microsoft Graph API's required operation. Other authentication flows (e.g., implicit grant flow or an on-behalf-of flow) can also be used to access the Microsoft Graph API.

Figure 6-1 is a diagram showing the sequence of events that happen when authenticating the Graph API using code grant flow authentication.

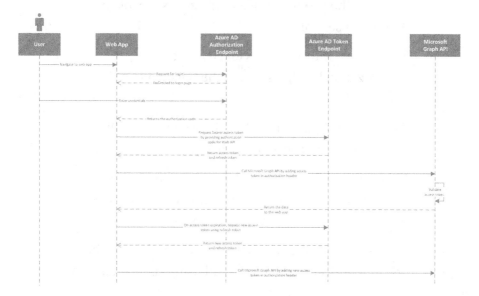

Figure 6-1. *Sequence diagram for Microsoft Graph API authentication using the code grant flow*

The following is the sequence of events performed during authentication.

1. The user navigates to the web application.

2. The web application redirects the user to the login page provided by Azure AD.

3. The user enters credentials and submits the sign-in request to the Azure Active Directory authorization endpoint.

4. On successful validation of the credentials, the Azure AD authorization endpoint returns the authorization code.

5. The web app requests the request bearer access token and refresh token from the Azure AD token endpoint using the authorization code. After receiving the tokens, the web app caches the tokens in the user session.

6. The request with an access token in the authorization header is sent to the Microsoft Graph API.

7. On successful validation, the Microsoft Graph API returns the response to the web app.

8. If the access token is expired, the web app sends a request to the Azure AD token endpoint to fetch a new access token using the refresh token.

The diagram in Figure 6-2 shows the sequence of events that happen when authenticating the Graph API using client credential flow authentication.

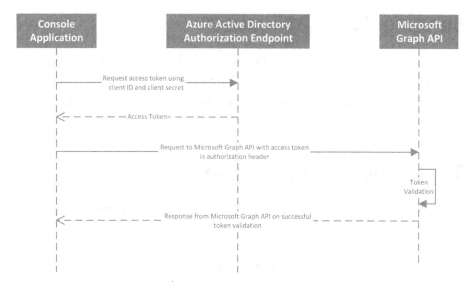

Figure 6-2. *Sequence diagram for Microsoft Graph API authentication using client credential flow*

The following is the sequence of events performed during authentication.

1. As soon as the background process starts, the request is sent to Azure AD with a client ID and a client secret to get an access token.

2. The request with an access token in the authorization header is sent to the Microsoft Graph API.

3. The Microsoft Graph API is secured by Azure Active Directory authentication, which validates the token.

4. On successful validation, a response is returned to call the application.

Running Your Application

To run your application and call the Microsoft Graph API, the first step is to register your app with Azure AD. You need to give delegate access to the Microsoft Graph API. Please follow the steps in the next section to configure your app in Azure.

Registering Your Application

Please follow these steps to register a console app with Azure AD.

1. Go to `https://portal.azure.com`.

2. Go to Azure Active Directory in the left navigation pane.

3. Click App Registrations.

4. Click New Registration.

5. Enter the name of your app.

6. Click Register.

7. Copy the application ID. It is the client ID of your application and required for token validation.

8. Click API Permission, and then click Add a Permission.

9. Click Microsoft Graph and select Application Permission.

10. Choose the required permissions. For the user, it is **User.ReadWrite.All**. This is similar for other resource types.

11. Grant administration consent by clicking the Grant
     Admin Consent button.

12. Generate a client secret. Go to Certificate and
     Secrets ➤ New Client Secret ➤ Give Description
     and Duration. Click the Add button. Copy the key
     and save it at a secured place. This key is not visible
     after you close this tile.

Our application is ready to read and update in Microsoft Azure
AD. Now let's create a console app.

Creating a Console Application

After registering your application, follow these steps to create a console
application.

1. Create a console application by using the .NET
    Framework.

2. Install the Microsoft.IdentityModel.Clients.Active
    Directory package from NuGet (www.nuget.org).

3. Add variables to configure the console app and to
    get an access token, as shown next.

```
private static string aadInstance = "https://login.
microsoftonline.com/{0}";
        private static string tenant = "tenant_id";
        private static string clientId = "client_id";
        private static string clientSecret = "client_
        secret";
    static string authority = String.Format(CultureInfo.
    InvariantCulture, aadInstance, tenant);
```

```
        private static string resourceId = "https://
        graph.microsoft.com";
    private static string graphAPIUrl = "https://graph.
    microsoft.com";
```

4. Add a method to generate a token for the Graph API, as shown next.

```
public static string GetAccessTokenForGraphAPI
(string clientId, string clientSecret, string
resourceId, string authority)
        {
            var autheContext = new AuthenticationContext
            (authority);
            ClientCredential clientCredential = new
            ClientCredential(clientId, clientSecret);
    var authResult = autheContext.
    AcquireTokenAsync(resourceId, clientCredential).Result;
            return authResult.AccessToken;
        }
```

The next step is to call the Microsoft Graph API to do the operation.

Calling Microsoft Graph to the Extend Resource Instance

As discussed, that resource instance can be extended using open extensions and schema extensions. API URLs and syntax are nearly the same for all the resources, such as users, groups, organization, and so forth. Here we explain the schema extension in the context of the user.

Open Extensions

By using open extensions, untyped data can be directly added to the resource instance. Custom data added through custom extensions can be accessed using the extensions navigation property of the resource instance. The extensionName property is a predefined property, and the name should be unique in the tenant.

Microsoft recommends naming a property name by using the reverse domain, such as com.your_domain.propertyName. If you want to add a property birth date, for example, then the name of the property should be com.your_domain_birthDate.

Let's proceed with a CRUD (create read update delete) operation for an extension property called birthDate.

Create

To create an open extension on the user, send a POST request to Microsoft Graph, as shown next.

```
public static bool AddOpenExtension(string userId, DateTime
birthDate, string extensionName, string accessToken)
    {
        string jsonString = $"{{ \"@odata.
        type\":\"microsoft.graph.openTypeExtension\",
        \"extensionName\":\"{extensionName}\",\"date\":
        \"{birthDate.ToShortDateString()}\"}}";
        HttpClient client = new HttpClient();
        HttpRequestMessage request = new HttpRequest
        Message(HttpMethod.Post, graphAPIUrl + $"/v1.0/
        users/{userId}/extensions");
        request.Content = new StringContent(jsonString,
        Encoding.UTF8, "application/json");
```

```
request.Headers.Authorization = new
AuthenticationHeaderValue("Bearer",
accessToken);
HttpResponseMessage response = client.
SendAsync(request).Result;

string responseResult = string.Empty;
if (response.IsSuccessStatusCode)
{
    Console.WriteLine(response.Content.
    ReadAsStringAsync().Result);
    return true;
}

return false;
    }
```

This method takes the user ID (the user object ID in Microsoft AD), the value of the extension property, the extension name, and the access token as input. It sends the POST request to Microsoft Graph v1 at https://graph.microsoft.com/v1.0/{userId}/extensions. If the request is successful, then it returns the status as 201.

Read

To read an open extension on the user, send a GET request to Microsoft Graph, as shown next.

```
public static bool ReadOpenExtension(string userId, string
extensionName, string accessToken)
    {
        HttpClient client = new HttpClient();
        HttpRequestMessage request = new HttpRequestMessage
        (HttpMethod.Get, graphAPIUrl + $"/v1.0/users/
        {userId}/extensions/{extensionName}");
```

```
request.Headers.Authorization = new Authentication
HeaderValue("Bearer", accessToken);
HttpResponseMessage response = client.SendAsync
(request).Result;

string responseResult = string.Empty;
if (response.IsSuccessStatusCode)
{
    Console.WriteLine(response.Content.ReadAsString
    Async().Result);
    return true;
}

return false;
}
```

This method takes the user ID (user object ID in Microsoft AD), the extension name, and the access token as input. It sends the GET request to Microsoft Graph v1 at https://graph.microsoft.com/v1.0/{userId}/extensions/{extensionName}. If the request is successful, then it returns the status as 200; in the body, the value of the open extension is returned.

Update

To update an open extension for the user, send a PATCH request to Microsoft Graph, as shown next.

```
public static bool UpdateOpenExtension(string userId, DateTime
birthDate, string extensionName, string accessToken)
        {
            string jsonString = $"{{ \"date\":\"{birthDate.
            ToShortDateString()}\"}}";
            HttpClient client = new HttpClient();
            var method = new HttpMethod("PATCH");
```

```
HttpRequestMessage request = new HttpRequestMessage
(method, graphAPIUrl + $"/v1.0/users/{userId}/
extensions/{extensionName}");
request.Content = new StringContent(jsonString,
Encoding.UTF8, "application/json");
request.Headers.Authorization = new Authentication
HeaderValue("Bearer", accessToken);
HttpResponseMessage response = client.SendAsync
(request).Result;

string responseResult = string.Empty;
if (response.IsSuccessStatusCode)
{
    return true;
}

return false;
}
```

This method takes the user ID (user object ID in Microsoft AD), the value of the extension property, the extension name, and the access token as input. It sends the PATCH request to Microsoft Graph v1 at https://graph.microsoft.com/v1.0/{userId}/extensions/{extensionName}. If the request is successful, then it returns the status as 204 without any content.

Delete

To delete an open extension for the user, send a DELETE request to Microsoft Graph, as shown next.

```
public static bool DeleteOpenExtension(string userId, string
extensionName, string accessToken)
```

```
{
    HttpClient client = new HttpClient();
    HttpRequestMessage request = new HttpRequestMessage
    (HttpMethod.Delete, graphAPIUrl + $"/v1.0/users/
    {userId}/extensions/{extensionName}");
    request.Headers.Authorization = new Authentication
    HeaderValue("Bearer", accessToken);
    HttpResponseMessage response = client.SendAsync
    (request).Result;

    string responseResult = string.Empty;
    if (response.IsSuccessStatusCode)
    {
        return true;
    }

    return false;
}
```

This method takes the user ID (user object ID in Microsoft AD),
extension name, and access token as input. It sends the DELETE request
to Microsoft Graph v1 at https://graph.microsoft.com/v1.0/{userId}/
extensions/{extensionName}. If the request is successful, then it returns
the status as 204 and deletes the open extension.

Schema Extensions

With schema extensions, schema data can be added to the resource type,
and then strongly typed custom data can be added to the resource instance
by using a defined schema. Typed data helps with filtering, authorization,
input validation, and so forth.

A schema extension definition ID should be unique in the tenant. Microsoft recommends two ways to define the ID.

- If you have your registered domain, then your ID should be domain_schemaName.

- If you don't have a domain, then your ID is your schemaName. Microsoft Graph automatically prepends it with a random eight characters and _. It looks like this: Jhdscvbf_schemaName.

Before executing a CRUD (create read update delete) operation on a schema extension, we need to add a schema. Also, deleting is not possible in a schema extension for a resource instance; you need to mark the extension property as null. Let's look at an example of adding vehicle information that is owned by a user. Vehicle information can have the following attributes: type, color, fuel type, and so forth.

Adding a Schema

A schema can be defined in resources as a user, group, organization, and so forth. The application that defines the schema acts as the owner of the schema. A schema internally maintains three states.

- **InDevelopment**. The initial state of the schema extension. Another app can use it provided it is in the same directory.

- **Available**. After development is complete, the owner can mark the state as available so that other applications can use it.

- **Deprecated**. If a schema extension is no longer valid, then the owner can mark it as deprecated. The schema extension is no longer available for read, update, or delete operations. Apps are still able to update the schema extension value for resource instances.

The state can only be changed by the owner of the application.

To Define the schema, Let's take an example of a user who owns a vehicle. We will store the vehicle information which is owned by user. Before defining the schema for vehicle information, let's look at the data types supported by the schema extension.

- **Binary**. Max limit is 256 bytes

- **Boolean**. True or false

- **DateTime**. Stores value in UTC in ISO 8601 format

- **Integer**. 32-bit integer

- **String**. Max limit is 256 characters

To create a schema extension on a user instance, send a POST request to Microsoft Graph, as shown next.

```
public static bool CreateSchema(string schemaName, string
accessToken, string clientId)
        {
                string jsonString = $"{{ \"id\":\"{schemaName}\",\"
                description\":\"Vehicle Information owned by user\",
                \"targetTypes\":[\"User\"],\"status\":\
                "InDevelopment\",\"owner\":\"{clientId}\",
                \"properties\":[{{\"name\":\"vehicleType\",
                \"type\":\"String\"}},{{\"name\":\"color\",\"type\":
                \"String\"}},{{\"name\":\"fuelType\",\"type\":
                \"String\"}}]}}";
                HttpClient client = new HttpClient();
```

```
HttpRequestMessage request = new HttpRequestMessage
(HttpMethod.Post, graphAPIUrl + "/v1.0/
schemaExtensions");
request.Content = new StringContent(jsonString,
Encoding.UTF8, "application/json");
request.Headers.Authorization = new Authentication
HeaderValue("Bearer", accessToken);
HttpResponseMessage response = client.SendAsync
(request).Result;

string responseResult = string.Empty;
if (response.IsSuccessStatusCode)
{
    Console.WriteLine(response.Content.
    ReadAsStringAsync().Result);
    return true;
}

return false;
}
```

This method takes the schema name, access token, and client ID (the owner) as input. It sends the POST request to Microsoft Graph v1 at https://graph.microsoft.com/v1.0/schemaExtensions. If the request is successful, then it returns the status as 201, and the schema is created on the user resource type.

Add-Update Schema Extension Value

To add or update the schema extension value for a resource instance, send a PATCH request to Microsoft Graph, as shown next.

```
public static bool AddUpdateSchemaExtensionValue
(string schemaName, string accessToken, string
verhicleType, string color, string fuelType, string
userId)
{
    string jsonString = $"{{\"{schemaName}\":{{\"vehicle
    Type\":\"{verhicleType}\",\"color\":\"{color}\",
    \"fuelType\":\"{fuelType}\"}}}}";
    HttpClient client = new HttpClient();
    var method = new HttpMethod("PATCH");
    HttpRequestMessage request = new HttpRequestMessage
    (method, graphAPIUrl + $"/v1.0/users/{userId}");
    request.Content = new StringContent(jsonString,
    Encoding.UTF8, "application/json");
    request.Headers.Authorization = new Authentication
    HeaderValue("Bearer", accessToken);
    HttpResponseMessage response = client.
    SendAsync(request).Result;

    string responseResult = string.Empty;
    if (response.IsSuccessStatusCode)
    {
        return true;
    }

    return false;
}
```

This method takes the schema name, access token, user ID (user object ID in Microsoft AD), and the value of various parameters of the schema extension as input. It sends the PATCH request to Microsoft Graph v1 at https://graph.microsoft.com/v1.0/users/{userId}. If the request is successful, then it returns the status as 204 without any content.

Read Schema Extension Value

To read a schema extension value on a user instance, send a GET request
to Microsoft Graph, as shown next.

```
public static bool ReadSchemaExtension(string userId, string
extensionName, string accessToken)
        {
            HttpClient client = new HttpClient();
            HttpRequestMessage request = new HttpRequestMessage
            (HttpMethod.Get, graphAPIUrl + $"/v1.0/users/
            {userId}?$select=id,{schemaName}");
            request.Headers.Authorization = new Authentication
            HeaderValue("Bearer", accessToken);
            HttpResponseMessage response = client.SendAsync
            (request).Result;

            string responseResult = string.Empty;
            if (response.IsSuccessStatusCode)
            {
                Console.WriteLine(response.Content.ReadAsString
                Async().Result);
                return true;
            }

            return false;
        }
```

This method takes the user ID (user object ID in Microsoft AD),
extension name, and access token as input. It sends the GET request to
Microsoft Graph v1 at https://graph.microsoft.com/v1.0/users/{user
Id}?$select=id,{schemaName}. If the request is successful, then it returns
the status code as 200 and in the body, ID and value of schema extension.

Remove Schema Extension Value

A schema extension value can't be deleted from a resource instance; it can only be marked as null. To mark the value as null for a schema extension for the user, send a PATCH request to Microsoft Graph, as shown next.

```
public static bool RemoveSchemaExtensionValue(string
schemaName, string accessToken, string userId)
        {
            string jsonString = $"{{\"{schemaName}\": null}}";
            HttpClient client = new HttpClient();
            var method = new HttpMethod("PATCH");
            HttpRequestMessage request = new HttpRequestMessage
            (method, graphAPIUrl + $"/v1.0/users/{userId}");
            request.Content = new StringContent(jsonString,
            Encoding.UTF8, "application/json");
            request.Headers.Authorization = new Authentication
            HeaderValue("Bearer", accessToken);
            HttpResponseMessage response = client.SendAsync
            (request).Result;

            string responseResult = string.Empty;
            if (response.IsSuccessStatusCode)
            {
                return true;
            }

            return false;
        }
```

This method takes the schema name, access token, and user ID (user object ID in Microsoft AD) as input. It sends the PATCH request to Microsoft Graph v1 at `https://graph.microsoft.com/v1.0/users/{userId}`. If the request is successful, it returns the status as 204 without any content, and marks the value of the schema extension property as null.

Note   The full code related to custom data extensions has been uploaded to GitHub and can be accessed at `https://github.com/aadfordevelopers/AadDemos/tree/master/CustomDataExtensions`. The same code can be extended for other resource types as well. Syntaxes remain same.

Summary

This chapter covered how to extend a resource instance with custom data using Microsoft Graph and OAuth 2.0 authentication flows. You learned how to extend custom data using open extensions and schema extensions. In the next chapter, we discuss how to invite and authenticate external users with Azure AD B2B.

CHAPTER 7

Authenticating External Users

In previous chapters, we discussed how a user can authenticate with Azure AD and access different types of applications (or resources) secured by Azure AD. In all such applications, the user was a valid registered user in the same Azure AD tenant, and in which the application being accessed was registered as well.

There could be scenarios in which you might want to provide access to users who are not registered with the application's Azure AD tenant. These users are categorized under B2B integration, in which users at another enterprise are trying to access an application. These users have a valid account with another domain service.

Based on the type of user defined, Azure AD provides another service—Azure AD B2B. In this chapter, we discuss the following in detail.

- Azure Active Directory B2B

- Configuring Azure AD for B2B collaboration

- Setting up our solution

- Configuring to support a guest inviter

- Adding a partner user as a guest inviter

- Adding Google as an identity provider

© Manas Mayank and Mohit Garg 2019
M. Mayank and M. Garg, *Developing Applications with Azure Active Directory*,
https://doi.org/10.1007/978-1-4842-5040-2_7

- Sending an invitation to the end user

- Configuring code

Azure Active Directory B2B

Azure Active Directory B2B supports users from another domain to access the resources secured by Azure Active Directory. Please note that an Azure AD Premium P1 or P2 license is needed to fully utilize the features mentioned in this section. Refer to MSDN to enable a trial version of Azure AD Premium. The following are the key features of Azure B2B.

- The organization owns the resource, or the application wants to provide access to external users to a specific resource. The user can be an independent individual with his or her own personal account or can be an employee of a partner organization with an account in the organization's directory service.

- Azure B2B works on invitation and redemption, rather than integrating using standards like OAuth or federation. Users are sent a request to access an application, and they access it after redeeming the request. Users are added to the tenant of the resource owner and access applications in the same manner as other users. Note that users are added as guest users in the AAD tenant.

- The partner accounts are managed by their identity provider. The policies for the user are defined by the identity provider.

- The users are provided access through a portal or PowerShell, or they can sign up themselves by using a custom-built self-service portal. Building a self-service portal is beyond the scope of this book. The code for it, however, is at the following GitHub repository: `https://github.com/Azure/active-directory-dotnet-graphapi-b2bportal-web`.

Configuring Azure AD for B2B Collaboration

We will look at how to use B2B collaboration through an example scenario. Let's consider the following scenario.

The admin from a resource owner tenant (let's call it an *enterprise tenant*) wants to share her resource applications with contracted users at another organization. The admin from the enterprise tenant delegates the addition of a new user to a user at the partner tenant. The partner organization uses another Azure AD tenant as their identity provider (let's call this a *partner tenant*). The application also allows Google to be used as the identity provider. The application involved is an MVC application calling a Web API (the application uses an authorization code grant flow). Let's start by creating an enterprise AD tenant and a partner AD tenant.

1. Go to the Azure portal. In the navigation pane, click Create a Resource.

2. In the search box, type **Azure Active Directory** and select the same option.

3. On the blade displayed, click the Create button. Enter the relevant details and click Create. We are creating a couple of tenants for our scenario: an enterprise tenant (azureadfordevsenterprise. onmicrosoft.com) and a partner tenant (azureadfordevspartner.onmicrosoft.com).

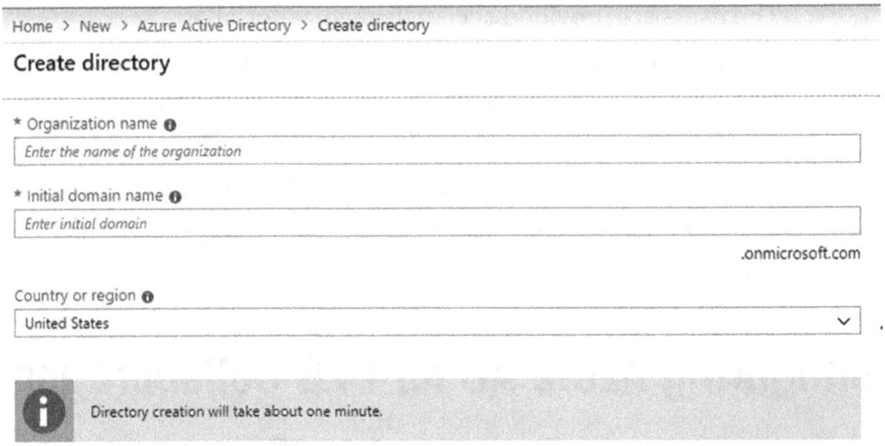

Figure 7-1. *Creating Azure AD tenants*

4. Go to the partner tenant and create a
    user in the partner tenant: (partneruser@
    azureadfordevspartner.onmicrosoft.com). This
    partner tenant user will be inviting other guests.

Setting up Our Solution

We will create applications using Visual Studio and register the same in our
enterprise tenant. We will use authorization code grant flow. Our solution
will contain three projects: an MVC web app trying to access APIs in a Web
API project, and a library containing code specific to Azure AD settings.

1. Go to Visual Studio and create a new project. Select
    the ASP.NET Core Web Application template. Name
    the project EnterpriseApp. Rename the solution
    created to AzureADEnterprise.

2. In the New ASP.NET Core Web Application pop-up window, select the project type API and click the Change Authentication button. This displays the Change Authentication dialog.

3. Select the "Work or School Accounts" option. In the drop-down menu, select Cloud – Single Organization. Enter the name of the enterprise tenant in the Domain field and press OK.

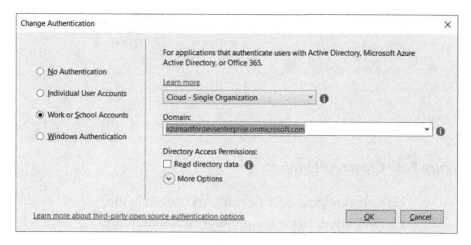

Figure 7-2. *Change authentication for project*

4. Press OK in the main projection creation dialog.

5. Similarly, create an MVC web app by choosing the Web Application (Model-View-Controller) option in the dialog (see Figure 7-3). Let's name our MVC project AppUI.

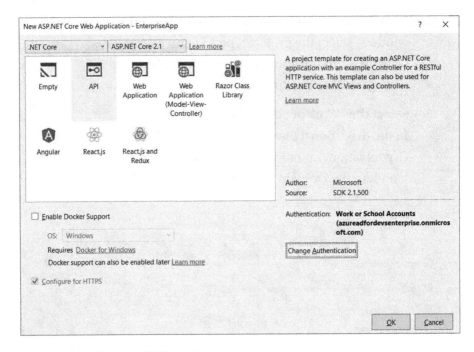

Figure 7-3. *Create API project*

6. Let's also create a .NET Core library project in the same solution. Name the project CommonLibrary.

7. We will come back to modifying our code at a later stage. For now, go to your Azure enterprise tenant, and then go to the Azure Active Directory service. Go to App Registrations under the Manage section. Notice that the applications that we created in the preceding steps are listed here. The name of the applications seen in Figure 7-4 were changed manually in the Azure portal.

Figure 7-4. *Applications registered on Azure tenant*

Configuring to Support a Guest Inviter

A guest inviter is a user from a partner tenant who has the rights to invite other users to use the resources. We will use the partner user we created earlier. Follow these steps to support users from a partner tenant.

1. Go to Azure portal ➤ Users ➤ User settings ➤
   Manage external collaboration settings.

Figure 7-5. *Accessing external collaboration settings*

2. Update the settings, as shown in Figure 7-6. These
    settings ensure that users with a "guest inviter" role
    can send invitations.

3. Set "Guest users permissions are limited" to No.
    This allows users from other domains (guest users)
    to have elevated rights. Set "Admins and users in the
    guest inviter role can invite" to Yes.

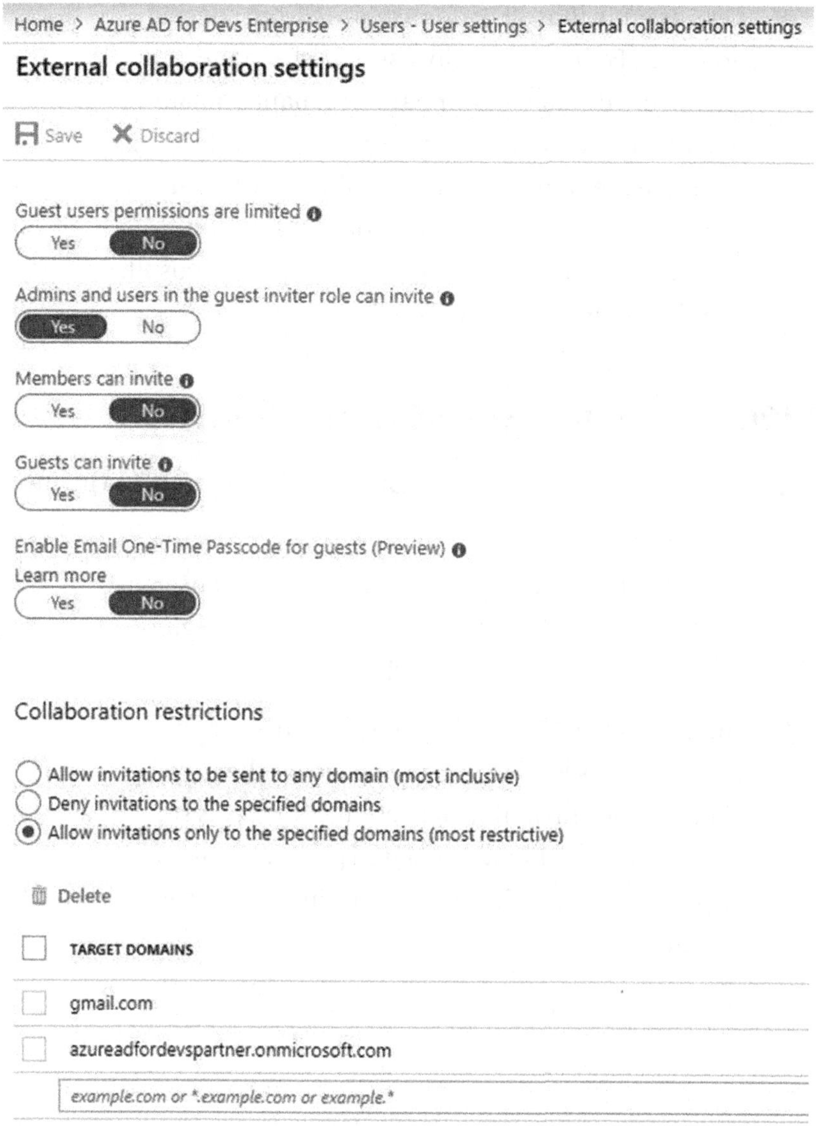

Figure 7-6. *External collaboration settings*

4. Let's assume that all of our users are from specific domains. For our scenario, users are from the gmail.com domain or our partner tenant domain (azureadfordevspartner.onmicrosoft.com). To mandate the same, choose the "Allow invitations only to the specified domains" option and add gmail.com and azureadfordevspartner.onmicrosoft.com (as shown in Figure 7-6). Press Save.

Adding a Partner User as a Guest Inviter

We will now add user from partner tenant and give her rights to invite other users.

1. Go to Users ➤ All Users and click New guest user. In the New Guest User screen, add your partner guest inviter account and press Invite.

2. Go to Users ➤ All Users and click the user created in step 1. This loads the profile page for the user. Initially, the "Invitation accepted" property is set to No. Update other user-related properties as applicable. Select "Directory role" in the Manage submenu.

***Figure 7-7.** Partner user settings*

3. On the Directory Role page, click the "Add assignment" button. This shows the Directory Roles menu. Select the "Guest inviter" role and press the Select button. This assigns the selected role to the user.

	Conditional Access administrator	Can manage conditional access capabilities.
	Customer LockBox access approver	Can approve Microsoft support requests to access customer organizational da
	Desktop Analytics administrator	Can access and manage Desktop management tools and services.
	Dynamics 365 administrator	Can manage all aspects of the Dynamics 365 product.
	Exchange administrator	Can manage all aspects of the Exchange product.
	External Identity Provider administr	Can configure identity providers for use in direct federation.
	Global administrator	Can manage all aspects of Azure AD and Microsoft services that use Azure AD
✓	Guest inviter	Can invite guest users independent of the 'members can invite guests' setting
	Helpdesk (Password) administrator	Can reset passwords for non-administrators and Helpdesk (Password) Adminis
	Information Protection administrate	Can manage all aspects of the Azure Information Protection product.
	Intune administrator	Can manage all aspects of the Intune product.
	License administrator	Ability to assign, remove and update license assignments.
	Message center reader	Can read messages and updates for their organization in Office 365 Message
	Power BI administrator	Can manage all aspects of the Power BI product.

Select

Figure 7-8. *Adding a guest inviter role to partner user*

4. Go to the enterprise tenant. Under Azure AD,
   select Enterprise applications ➤ All applications ➤
   Enterprise API ➤ Users and groups. Click the Add
   user button. In the Add Assignment blade, select
   Users and groups.

5. Search for the partner user added in step 1 and press
   Select. This adds the partner user to the application.

6. Repeat steps 4 and 5 for the MVC application.

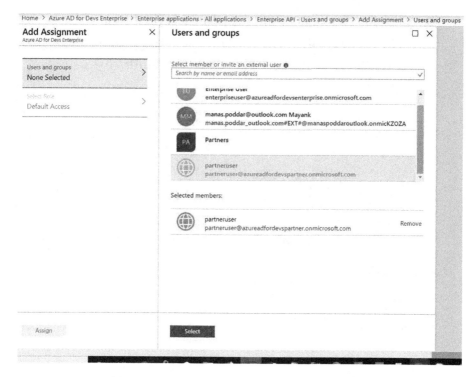

Figure 7-9. *Adding a partner user*

7. Go to https://account.activedirectory.
    windowsazure.com/r. Log in with the partner
    user credentials by using a fully qualified name
    (partneruser@azureadfordevspartner.onmicrosoft.
    com). This displays the My Apps or the Access panel
    of the current user, which the user has access to
    within her organization. Please refer to https://
    docs.microsoft.com/en-us/azure/active-
    directory/user-help/my-apps-portal-end-user-
    overview for further information.

8. Click the username of the signed-in user (in the top-right corner) and notice the Organizations section in the menu; both the partner and the enterprise AD are displayed.

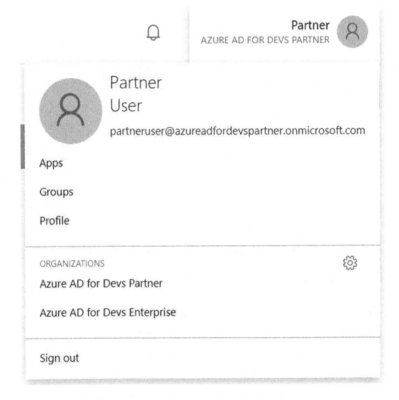

Figure 7-10. *Partner user access panel login*

9. Select Azure AD for Devs Enterprise. Notice that both the Enterprise API and the Enterprise UI are displayed. The application may not immediately appear on the access panel. Sign off and sign back in on a different browser instance if this happens.

Figure 7-11. *Partner user's access panel*

10. Hover over the application name and click the three dots menu. Notice that the Manage Apps option is available for both applications.

We have configured the partner user to allow her to add other users of the application. We will come back to adding end users, but before we do that, we need to add other settings and configure our code. In addition, the "Invitation accepted" property is now set to Yes. These configurations allow the partner user to send invitations to other users.

Adding Google as an Identity Provider

The partner user can now invite other users to access the applications. Azure AD allows users to authenticate using Google as an identity provider. This allows partner users to send invitations to Gmail users. The invited Gmail users can use their Google credentials to sign in. The following are the steps needed to add Google as an identity provider.

1. Go to `https://console.developers.google.com` and log in with Google credentials. This lands on a dashboard page. Create a new project for integrating with Azure AD B2B by clicking the Create button. Enter the name of the project, **AzureADB2B**, and create a new project.

2. Select the project and go to its dashboard.

3. Go to the Credentials tab and select the "OAuth client ID" option from the "Create credentials" drop-down menu.

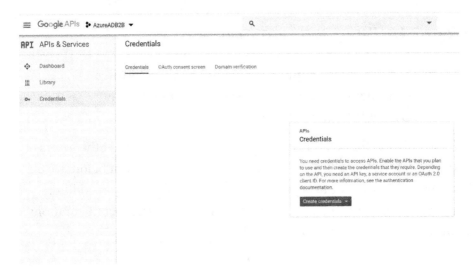

Figure 7-12. *Google create credentials*

4. Click the "Configure consent screen" button.

Figure 7-13. *Google configure consent*

5. On the Credentials screen, enter the name of the application and other details. In the "Authorized domains" field, enter **microsoftonline.com**. Click the Save button.

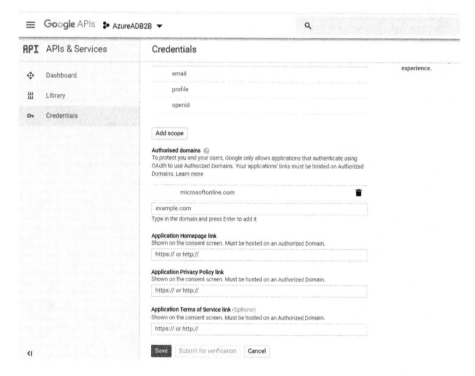

Figure 7-14.   Google enter credentials

6. On the "Create OAuth client ID" screen, select Web Application as the application type and add the following URLs in the "Authorized redirect URIs" section:

- **https://login.microsoftonline.com**

- **https://login.microsoftonline.com/ te/<tenant id>/oauth2/authresp**, where the tenant ID is Azure Active Directory

7.   Click the Create button.

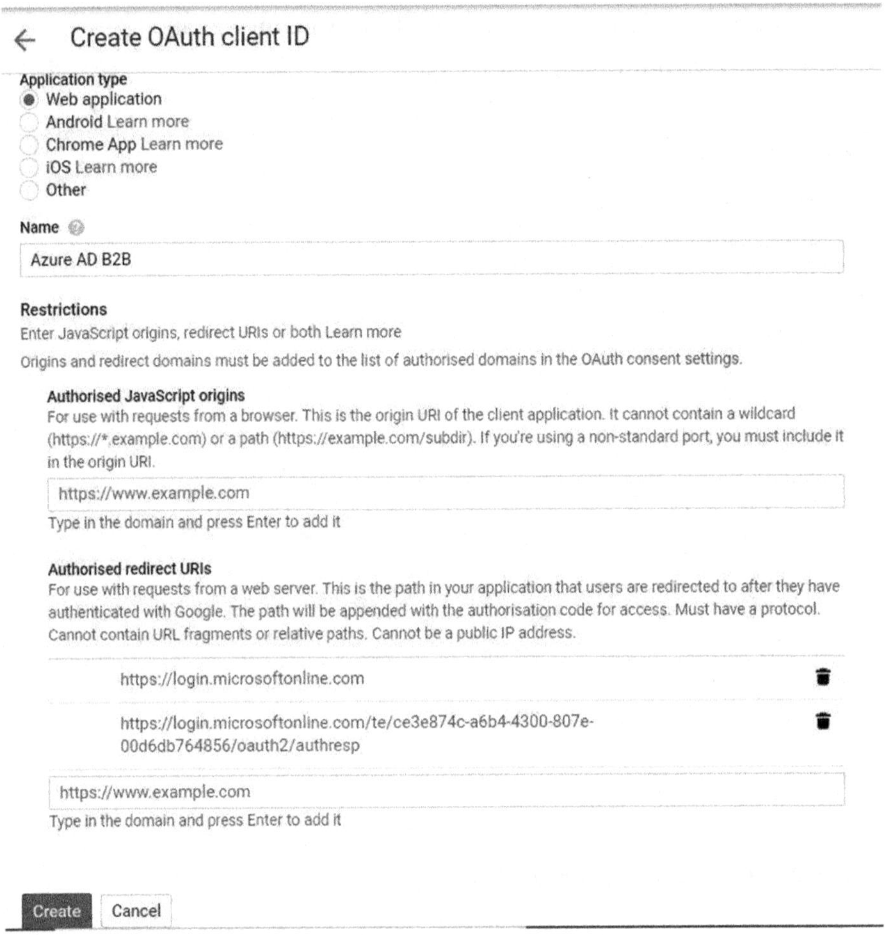

Figure 7-15. *Google create OAuth client*

8.   A prompt displays the client ID and the client secret. Copy this information.

9.   Go to Azure AD ➤ Organizational relationships ➤ Identity providers ➤ Google. Add the client ID and the client secret and click Save.

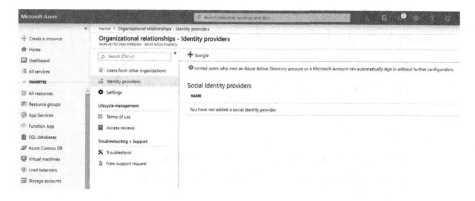

Figure 7-16. *Add Google as identity provider*

The Azure portal shows Google added as a social identity provider.

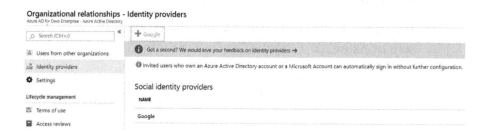

Figure 7-17. *Google added as identity provider*

Sending an Invitation to the End User

Let's send an invitation to our end user. We added a partner user to our
tenant as a guest inviter. This allows the partner user to send invitations
to external users. For this scenario, let's try sending the invitation to a user
with a Gmail ID.

213

1. Go back to the access panel and log in with the
    credentials of the partner user.

2. Click the API's three dots menu and go to Manage
    Apps. This loads the Apps page. Note that the users
    of the application are listed on the right side of the
    page.

3. Click the + icon displayed in the top right-hand
    corner of the page. This loads the "Add members"
    dialog.

4. In the search textbox, enter the Gmail user, and then
    click the Add button. This sends an invitation to the
    Gmail user.

5. Log in to the relevant Gmail account and go the mail
    sent by Azure AD. Click the Get Started button.

Figure 7-18. *Invitation mail for enterprise tenant*

6. Accept the review permissions. Users are redirected
    to their access panel. Users can go back to the
    panel at `https://account.activedirectory.`
    `windowsazure.com/r?tenantId=<tenand id>`,
    where tenant ID the tenant ID of enterprise Azure
    AD tenant.

The end user can now access the application. First, let's go back to our
code to get it up and running.

Configuring Code

The application will follow the authorization code grant flow. It will be in
line with the solution described in Chapter 3. Let's tweak the code for this
solution.

1. Go to Visual Studio and open the
    AzureADEnterprise.sln solution that you created
    previously.

2. Under the API project, find Startup.cs and
    change the authentication mechanism in the
    ConfigureServices method.

```
services.AddAuthentication(sharedOptions =>
        {
                sharedOptions.DefaultScheme =
                JwtBearerDefaults.AuthenticationScheme;
        })
        .AddJwtBearer(options =>
        {
                options.Audience = "<client-id>";
                options.Authority = "https://login.
                microsoftonline.com/<tenand-id>";
```

```
options.TokenValidationParameters = new
TokenValidationParameters
{
    ValidateIssuer = true,
    SaveSigninToken = true,
};
});
```

<client-id> is the application ID of the API
application and <tenant-id> is the tenant ID of the
enterprise Azure AD tenant.

3. Go to ValuesController.cs and change the default
    Get method. This method now just returns a string.

```
[HttpGet]
        public ActionResult<string> Get()
        {
            return "About link clicked!";
        }
```

4. Locate your MVC project and go to HomeController.
    Locate the About method and add the following code:

```
string userObjectID = (User.FindFirst("http://schemas.
microsoft.com/identity/claims/objectidentifier"))?.Value;
                AuthenticationContext authContext =
                new AuthenticationContext(AzureAd
                Options.Settings.Authority, new Token
                SessionCache(userObjectID, HttpContext.
                Session));
                ClientCredential credential = new
                ClientCredential(AzureAdOptions.
                Settings.ClientId, AzureAdOptions.
                Settings.ClientSecret);
```

```
            result = await authContext.Acquir
            eTokenSilentAsync(AzureAdOptions.
            Settings.ResourceId, credential,
            new UserIdentifier(userObjectID,
            UserIdentifierType.UniqueId));
HttpClient client = new HttpClient();
            HttpRequestMessage request = new Http
            RequestMessage(HttpMethod.Get, AzureAd
            Options. Settings.ResourceBasePath +
            "/api/values");
            request.Headers.Authorization = new Auth
            enticationHeaderValue("Bearer", result.
            AccessToken);
            HttpResponseMessage response = await
            client.SendAsync(request);
            ViewData["Message"] = await response.
            Content.ReadAsStringAsync();
```

We are calling the Get method of ValuesController
from our MVC controller. The rest of the code
remains the same as defined in the "Web App/Web
API Authentication" section in Chapter 3.

5. Run the application and log in with your Gmail
    credentials.

6. Click the About link on the home page. This calls
    the About method in the HomeController of the
    MVC app, which further calls the Get method of the
    ValuesController of the API app. This displays the
    string returned from the API.

Figure 7-19. End user's About page

Summary

In this chapter, you saw how to enable an Azure AD tenant to allow access to external users. You also enabled Google as an identity provider. You created an inviter for guest users. The flow that we defined is relevant to a single Azure AD tenant. In the next chapter, you learn how to enable users from multiple tenants to access your application.

CHAPTER 8

Multitenancy

In Chapter 7, we discussed how to utilize Azure AD to support external users by using Azure AD B2C and Azure AD B2B. We will continue our discussion on supporting external users of other Azure AD accounts. The users will be authenticated by their respective Azure AD tenant. We will do so by using multitenancy.

We cover the following topics in this chapter.

- Multitenancy models

- Setting up our solution

- Configuring a user from another AAD tenant

- Configuring an application to support multitenancy

- Configuring applications

- Restricting Azure AD tenants

- Multitenancy in an application

Before we get into other details, let's first discuss the meaning of multitenancy and its types.

© Manas Mayank and Mohit Garg 2019
M. Mayank and M. Garg, *Developing Applications with Azure Active Directory*,
https://doi.org/10.1007/978-1-4842-5040-2_8

Multitenancy Models

Most of the application examples that we investigated in previous chapters referred to a single tenant. In the context of Azure AD, this signified that users belonged to a single Azure AD instance or tenant. In most scenarios, this indicates that users belong to a single organization.

Multitenancy refers to a scenario in which users from a different organization use the same application instance. Multitenancy by itself is a broad topic and could address at the application level or the database level. The following are some multitenancy models.

- **A standalone application accessing a standalone database**. We create different sets of application and database combinations for different tenant organizations. Initial development efforts have fewer sets, but as the number of tenant organizations increase, it could become a nightmare from a maintenance perspective.

- **Applications with the same database for each tenant**. In this scenario, all the data for all the tenants are stored in the same set of database tables. The data is segregated at the row level by a key. This key uniquely signifies the tenants. This pattern is best in scenarios in which there are a significant number of tables with applicable common data, regardless of the tenants. Also, adding a new customer does not require significant effort from the database. This pattern is challenging to implement when converting existing single-tenant applications to support multitenancy. In addition, due to the size of some transactional tables, storing data for multiple tenants can quickly increase.

This pattern is not suitable if the data for each tenant needs to be physically segregated. Such requirements may be mandated from a security point of view.

- **Applications with the same database but a different set of tables for each tenant**. We can also write logic to dynamically interpret the set of tables applicable to each customer. Adding a new customer involves updating the same database with a new set of tables. The data is physically co-located and logically segregated by the tables.

- **Applications with a different database for each tenant**. The data is stored on a different database server for each customer. The schema for each customer can be independently customized. The data is fetched from a different database instance for every tenant. There could be performance implications due to changing the database connection for every request.

- **Hybrid approach**. This model entails a combination of the preceding approaches. For example, you might store data for multiple customers in the same tables. In addition, another set of customers could have data stored in a different database instance.

Azure AD supports multitenancy for the applications secured by it. The focus of this chapter is on authenticating users registered in different Azure AD tenants. These authenticated users will try to access the same set of applications that are registered on another Azure AD tenant. Let's start with configuring our application to explain multitenancy support in Azure AD.

Setting up Our Solution

Refer to the MVC and API apps described in Chapter 7. These applications were configured to run on a single tenant. After a user logs in, Azure AD issues an ID token to the MVC application. This token has a set of claims for the user. One of the claims, iss, refers to the tenant that issued the token (issuer). You can check the same by debugging the application when the authorization code is received by the MVC application, as indicated in the screenshot of code shown in Figure 8-1.

```
private async Task OnAuthorizationCodeReceived(AuthorizationCodeReceivedContext context)
{
    string userObjectId = (context.Principal.FindFirst("http://schemas.microsoft.com/identity/claims/objectidentifier"))?.Value;    ≤ 2.947ms elapsed
```
⊡ ⚲ context.JwtSecurityToken   [{"alg":"RS256","typ":"JWT","x5t":"HBxl9mAe6gxavCkcoOU2THsDNa0","kid
⊞ ⚲ context.JwtSecurityToken.Claims   Count = 21
⊞● new System.Collections.Generic.ICollectionDebugView<System.Security.Claims.Claim>(context.JwtSecurityToken.Claims).Items[1 {iss: https://sts.windows.net/ce3e874c-a6b4-4300-807e-00d6db764856/}

Figure 8-1. *iss claim for single tenant application*

This happens because our application is configured to authenticate users for a single tenant only. In the next, section we enable users from multiple Azure AD tenants to access the application. We need a user from another Azure AD tenant for this.

We will create code structure similar to what we did in the B2B scenario in Chapter 7. Our application has three projects: an MVC web app, an API app, and a library project. Create these using a Visual Studio template for creating an ASP.NET Core web application. The authentication should be set to the "Work or School Accounts" option. For now, let's choose Cloud – Single Organization. Use our previous Azure AD tenant: azureadfordevsenterprise.onmicrosoft.com. Name the projects MultitenantUI, MultitenantAPI, and CommonLibrary for the MVC web app, API app, and library project, respectively.

Figure 8-2. *Solution structure*

Configuring a User from Another AAD Tenant

We need to create a user in another Azure AD tenant.

1. Create another Azure AD tenant for a hypothetical partner organization (azureadfordevspartner. onmicrosoft.com), as discussed in the B2B flow in Chapter 7.

2. Switch to the new directory and add a new user (a partner user) in the new tenant.

Figure 8-3. *Create partner user*

A new user named partneruser is added to the tenant.

Configuring an Application to Support Multitenancy

We will extend our application to support users from a different Azure AD
tenant. Both applications (MVC and API) are registered in our enterprise
tenant (azureadfordevsenterprise.onmicrosoft.com). We will make
changes to allow a partner user to access these applications.

1. Go to the Azure AD enterprise account and search
    for your MVC application. Click the application.

2. Go to the Authentication option under the
    Manage menu.

3. In the window displayed, look for "Supported account types" and select the Accounts option in any organizational directory. This allows users from other Azure AD tenants to access the applications.

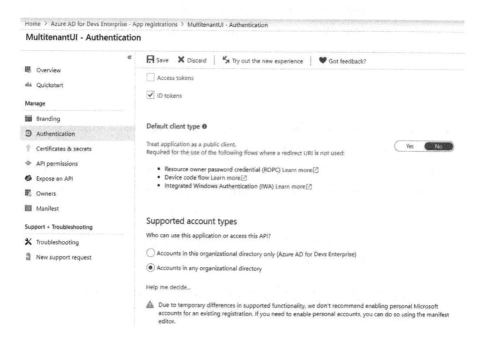

Figure 8-4. *Enable multitenancy*

4. Repeat the same set of steps for the API.

5. Switch back to your code and go to the OpenID Connect options (OpenIDConnectConfig.cs). In the Configure method, set the Authority option to `https://login.microsoftonline.com/common`.

```
public void Configure(string name, OpenIdConnectOptions
options)
{
        options.ClientId = azureADSettings.ClientId;
```

```
// Single tenant authority as used previously
// options.Authority = azureADSettings.Authority;
// Multi-tenant authority cannot be specific to a
   tenant instance, and should point to https://
   login.microsoftonline.com/common
options.Authority = "https://login.microsoftonline.
com/common";

...
}
```

In a single tenant scenario, we validate the user against a single AD instance and set this variable to a specific tenant (as in our previous single tenant): https://login.microsoftonline.com/<tenant-id>. In multitenancy, the user's Azure AD tenant is discovered during the time of user sign-in.

6. In this method, disable the token validating the issuer of the token.

    ```
    options.TokenValidationParameters.ValidateIssuer =
    false;
    ```

7. Try running the applications from Visual Studio and logging in with the partner user's credentials which were created earlier. You might encounter error, as seen in Figure 8-5.

Need admin approval

MultitenantUI

MultitenantUI needs permission to access resources in your organization that only an admin can grant. Please ask an admin to grant permission to this app before you can use it.

Have an admin account? Sign in with that account

Return to the application without granting consent

Figure 8-5. *Consent approval error*

This leads us to consent. We will make changes to get around this error.

Configuring the Applications

The earlier error clearly indicates that the application might access resources in a partner's tenant. Accessing some of these resources requires permissions from the admin.

1. Go to the main enterprise Azure AD tenant and search for your MVC application. Click the application.

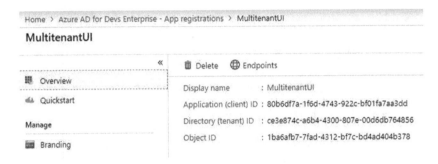

Figure 8-6. *IDs of the application*

2. Note the application ID (80b6df7a-1f6d-4743-922c-bf01fa7aa3dd) and object ID (1ba6afb7-7fad-4312-bf7c-bd4ad404b378) properties .

3. Under the Manage menu, click API permissions. Check for the permissions granted to the application. The blade has an "API permissions" grid that lists all the permissions. Click the individual permissions. The "Admin consent required" field indicates if the consent of the admin user is needed to access the resource. For all Graph API–related permissions, refer to `https://docs.microsoft.com/en-us/previous-versions/azure/ad/graph/howto/azure-ad-graph-api-permission-scopes` to find out if admin permission is needed to access that resource. In our scenario, the Directory.Read. All permission needs admin consent.

Figure 8-7. *API permissions*

4. There are couple of ways to enable access to our partner user. You can remove the Directory.Read. All permission and try to access the application for now. The rule of the thumb is to give an application the minimal amount of permissions that it needs. This is important from a security perspective. The other option is to sign in as an administrator to provide consent.

5. We will access the API from the web app under the user's context. In enterprise Azure AD, go to "App registrations". Click your MVC application and from the menu, select "API permissions". Click the "Add a permission" button, which opens a sidebar with the "Request API permissions" heading. Select "APIs my organization uses" and search for MultitenantAPI. Click the "Delegated permissions" tab, select the permission, and save.

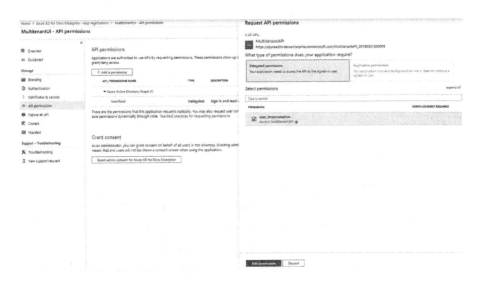

Figure 8-8. *Web-app delegated user*

6. Go to back to Partner Azure AD ➤ Enterprise
    Applications ➤ All Applications. Note that there are
    no applications added yet (given we created it for
    our example).

Figure 8-9. *Applications in a partner tenant*

7. Ensure that the user can consent. This can be done by going to Partner AD ➤ Enterprise Applications ➤ User settings. Set the "Users can consent to the apps accessing company data on their behalf" option to Yes.

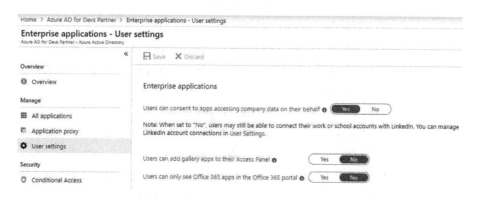

Figure 8-10. *Users allowed to consent*

8. Since the API application is always accessed through MVC, we can combine the consent approval by the partner users for both the API and MVC. To do so, go to our enterprise Azure AD tenant ➤ App Registrations. Click the MultitenantAPI application and select Manifest. The metadata for the API application is displayed in JSON format. Look for the key called knownClientApplications and set its value to the application ID of the MVC application. Click the Save button.

```
"knownClientApplications": ["80b6df7a-1f6d-4743-922c-
bf01fa7aa3dd"]
```

9. Repeat the same steps in the API for Azure AD. Add code that calls the API from the About method of HomeController.cs in the MVC project.

```
public async Task<IActionResult> About()
{
    string userObjectID = (User.FindFirst("http://
    schemas.microsoft.com/identity/claims/
    objectidentifier"))?.Value;
    // Single tenant authority
    // AuthenticationContext authContext = new Authe
    // nticationContext(AzureADSettings.AzureSettings.
    // Authority);
    // Multi-tenant authority cannot be specific to a
    // tenant instance, and should point to https://login.
    // microsoftonline.com/common
    AuthenticationContext authContext = new Authentication
    Context("https://login.microsoftonline.com/common");
    ClientCredential credential = new ClientCrede
    ntial(AzureADSettings.AzureSettings.ClientId,
    AzureADSettings.AzureSettings.ClientSecret);
    var result = await authContext.AcquireTokenAs
    ync(AzureADSettings.AzureSettings.ResourceId,
    credential);
    HttpClient client = new HttpClient();
    HttpRequestMessage request = new
    HttpRequestMessage(HttpMethod.Get, AzureADSettings.
    AzureSettings.ResourceBasePath + "/api/values");
    request.Headers.Authorization = new AuthenticationH
    eaderValue("Bearer", result.AccessToken);
    HttpResponseMessage response = await client.
    SendAsync(request);
    ViewData["Message"] = await response.Content.
    ReadAsAsync<string>();
    return View();
}
```

10. Run the applications again from Visual Studio and log in with the partner user. The application will show the user's consent screen.

Figure 8-11. *Request for consent*

11. Click the OK button to allow the user to log in to the application.

Figure 8-12. *Partner user logged in*

12. Go back to Partner AD ➤ Enterprise Applications ➤ All Applications. Note that our applications were added. In addition, pay attention to the application ID (80b6df7a-1f6d-4743-922c-bf01fa7aa3dd) and object ID (25aec4ea-c848-4132-b1b9-12fb2b67c4dc) properties. Compare these to the values in step 1. You will notice that the application ID value is the same in both places; but the values for the object ID are different. The application ID property refers to the application instance that was registered on the Azure AD tenant. When a partner user consents to an application, a representation of the application is created in the partner AD tenant. This representational object is denoted by the object ID and is called a *service principal.* A service principal is also created in the tenant in which the application was originally registered (enterprise tenant in our case).

Restricting the Azure AD Tenants

Note that in the preceding steps, we set `options.TokenValidationParameters.ValidateIssuer = false`. This ensures that our application will not validate the user's tenant. This setting allows users from any Azure AD tenant to access our application. In most scenarios, we only want to restrict application access from users from certain tenants.

Follow these steps to enable this.

1. Open your MVC code in Visual Studio. Go to the OpenID Connect options (`OpenIdConnectConfig.cs`) and set `options.TokenValidationParameters.ValidateIssuer = true`, in the Configure method.

2. OpenID Connect configurations provide a delegate that is utilized for validating the issuer.

```
public void Configure(string name, OpenIdConnectOptions options)
{
...
  options.TokenValidationParameters.ValidateIssuer = true;
  options.TokenValidationParameters.IssuerValidator = ValidateIssuer;
...
}
```

3. Add an implementation for the ValidateIssuer method.

```
private string ValidateIssuer(string issuer, SecurityToken, TokenValidationParameters validationParameters)
        {
                if (validIssuers.Contains(issuer?.ToLower Invariant()))
```

```
        {
            return issuer;
        }

        throw new SecurityTokenInvalidIssuer
        Exception($"Invalid tenant: {issuer}")
        {
            InvalidIssuer = issuer
        };
    }
```

validIssuers could be defined in the following code. In a real-world application, it should be populated through a database/configurations or another persistence mechanism.

```
private readonly List<string> validIssuers = new
List<string>()
{
    "https://sts.windows.net/ce3e874c-a6b4-4300-807e-
    00d6db764856/",
    "https://sts.windows.net/9ffc2d15-ffdd-4a44-9f6b-
    1b11df8bb417/"
};
```

If the issuer is not valid, we throw SecurityTokenInvalidIssuerException.

Multitenancy in an Application

In the previous section, we discussed how to set up a multitenant application in Azure AD. We also talked about various patterns for multitenancy. We will try to take the pattern of having different databases for each tenant and integrate it to Azure AD. The objective is to demonstrate how multitenant applications can leverage Azure AD. We will dynamically connect the database, depending on the tenant to which the user belongs. We will use the same solution as in earlier sections.

Let's start by creating very simple databases, one each for Enterprise and Partner. Let's call them EnterpriseDB and PartnerDB, respectively.

1. Create the same Employees table in both databases. Use the same script for both databases. Each table contains information about employees from each respective organization.

```
SET ANSI_NULLS ON
GO

SET QUOTED_IDENTIFIER ON
GO

CREATE TABLE [dbo].[Employees](
        [EmployeeId] [int] IDENTITY(1,1) NOT NULL,
        [FirstName] [nvarchar](50) NOT NULL,
        [SecondName] [nvarchar](50) NULL,
        [Department] [nvarchar](50) NULL,
 CONSTRAINT [PK_Employees] PRIMARY KEY CLUSTERED
 (
        [EmployeeId] ASC
)WITH (PAD_INDEX = OFF, STATISTICS_NORECOMPUTE = OFF,
IGNORE_DUP_KEY = OFF, ALLOW_ROW_LOCKS = ON, ALLOW_PAGE_
LOCKS = ON) ON [PRIMARY]
) ON [PRIMARY]
GO
```

2. Insert sample data in both tables.

	EmployeeId	FirstName	SecondName	Department
1	1	Mahendra	Kohli	Enterprise HR
2	2	Sachin	Dev	Enterprise Finance

Figure 8-13. *Employees table in Enterprise database*

3. Add similar data in the employees table of the partner tenant.

	EmployeeId	FirstName	SecondName	Department
1	1	Rahul	Srinath	Partner HR
2	2	Sunil	Ganguly	Partner Sales

Figure 8-14. *Employees table in Partner database*

4. We will use the EntityFramework Core (EF Core) database approach to access our database tables. In our API project, add a reference to EF Core–related NuGet packages.

```
Microsoft.EntityFrameworkCore.SqlServer
Microsoft.EntityFrameworkCore.SqlServer.Design
Microsoft.EntityFrameworkCore.Tools
```

5. Create a folder called DAL in the API project. From Visual Studio Server Explorer, connect to EnterpriseDB.

6. From the Visual Studio menu, select Tools ➤ NuGet Package Manger ➤ Package Manager Console. Run the following command.

```
PM> Scaffold-DbContext "Server=.;Database=
EnterpriseDB;Trusted_Connection=True;" Microsoft.
EntityFrameworkCore.SqlServer -OutputDir DAL
```

7. This generates Employees.cs with the Employees entity and a class for the database context, EnterpriseDBContext.cs.

```
public partial class Employees
    {
        public int EmployeeId { get; set; }
        public string FirstName { get; set; }
        public string SecondName { get; set; }
        public string Department { get; set; }
    }
```

8. Rename the EnterpriseDBContext class TenantDBContext. We will use the same database context object to access both databases. In TenantDBContext, add a method to get a list of all the employees from the database.

```
public async Task<List<Employees>> GetEmployees()
        {
            return await this.Employees.
            ToListAsync<Employees>();
        }
```

As explained earlier, we will change the database context (or the connection string), depending on the tenant that the user belongs to. To achieve this, we need a place to maintain this mapping with a tenant and a database connection string. Ideally, this should be done in a secure persistence, like Azure Key Vault.

For our purposes, let's create a class that holds the mapping between the tenant ID and the connection string; let's call this class TenantConnectionMapper. It exposes one method that returns the connection string on the basis of the tenant ID.

```
public class TenantConnectionMapper
    {
        // Dictionary holding the mapping between and AD tenant
        // and corresponding connection string.
        private readonly Dictionary<string, string>
        connectionMapper = new Dictionary<string, string>();

        public TenantConnectionMapper()
        {
            connectionMapper.Add("ce3e874c-a6b4-4300-807e-
            00d6db764856", "Server=.;Database=EnterpriseDB;
            Trusted_Connection=True;");
            connectionMapper.Add("9ffc2d15-ffdd-4a44-9f6b-
            1b11df8bb417", "Server=.;Database=PartnerDB;
            Trusted_Connection=True;");
        }

        // This is for demo purpose. In real world scenario
        // this method will get connection string from a secure
        // persistence.
        public string GetConnectionString(string tenant)
        {
            if (connectionMapper.Keys.Contains(tenant))
            {
                return connectionMapper[tenant];
            }
```

```
        return string.Empty;
    }
}
```

1. Add another class, DBConnectionFactory. This class
    is responsible for getting a database connection
    object (DBConnection) on the basis of the user's
    tenant ID. The tenant ID could be extracted from
    the claims in the user token. The user's claims can
    be extracted from each HTTP request by using
    HttpContextAccessor, as mentioned in the following
    code.

```
public class DBConnectionFactory
    {
        private readonly IHttpContextAccessor httpContext
        Accessor;
        private readonly TenantConnectionMapper tenant
        ConnectionMapper;
        public DBConnectionFactory(IHttpContextAccess
        or httpContextAccessor, TenantConnectionMapper
        tenantConnectionMapper)
        {
            this.httpContextAccessor = httpContext
            Accessor;
            this.tenantConnectionMapper = tenant
            ConnectionMapper;
        }
```

```
public DbConnection GetDbConnection()
{
    var tenantId = httpContextAccessor.
    HttpContext.User.Claims
.FirstOrDefault(x => x.Type == "http://
schemas.microsoft.com/identity/claims/
tenantid")?.Value;
    string connectionString = this.
    tenantConnectionMapper.
    GetConnectionString(tenantId);
    return new SqlConnection(connectionString);
}
}
```

2. This method exposes a method called GetDbConnection; the purpose of this method is to get the connection string from TenantConnectionMapper, depending on the tenant.

3. Go back to the TenantDBContext class and add a constructor, which accepts the connectionFactory object and assigns it to a variable.

```
private readonly DBConnectionFactory connectionFactory;
        public TenantDBContext(DBConnectionFactory
        connectionFactory)
        {
            this.connectionFactory = connectionFactory;
        }
```

4. Change the OnConfiguring method as follows. This enables the database context to be set dynamically during runtime from the connection factory.

```
protected override void OnConfiguring(DbContextOptions
Builder optionsBuilder)
        {
            if (!optionsBuilder.IsConfigured)
            {
                optionsBuilder.UseSqlServer(this.
                connectionFactory.GetDbConnection());
            }
        }
```

5. In your API's startup class, go to the ConfigureServices method and register the following types.

```
services.AddSingleton<IHttpContextAccessor,
HttpContextAccessor>();
            services.AddSingleton<TenantConnection
            Mapper>();
            services.AddTransient<DBConnectionFactory>();
            services.AddTransient<TenantDBContext>();
```

6. Go to ValuesController and change the default Get.

```
[HttpGet]
public async Task<ActionResult<string>> Get()
{
        var token = this.HttpContext.Request.Headers
        ["Authorization"];
    var employees = await dbContext.GetEmployees();
    return  "About link clicked. Found employees:
" + string.Join(", ", employees?.Select(x =>    x.
FirstName + " " + x.SecondName)) ;
}
```

7. Ensure that you inject a database context object to the constructor of your controller.

```
public ValuesController(TenantDBContext dbContext)
    {
        this.dbContext = dbContext;
    }
```

8. Call this controller method by clicking the About link in your UI, as you did in Chapter 7. Run the application from Visual Studio.

9. Log in as a partner user and click the About link. You will notice the employees of the partner tenant listed on the UI.

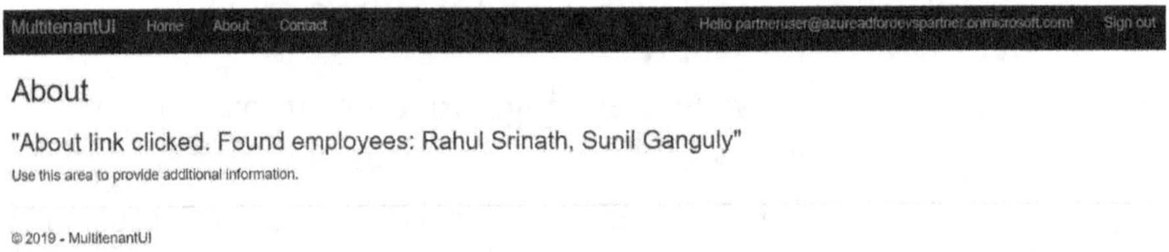

Figure 8-15. *Employees in the PartnerDB*

Sign in as an enterprise user and click the About link to get data from EnterpriseDB and display it on the UI.

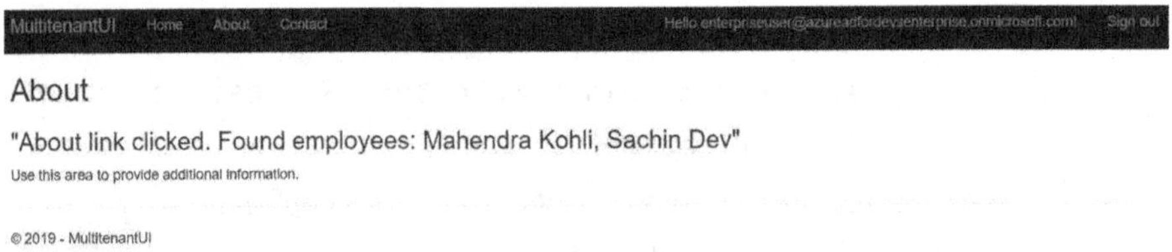

Figure 8-16. *Employees in the EnterpriseDB*

We conceptually demonstrated how our applications can leverage the multitenancy feature in Azure AD. The same concepts are applicable to other patterns of multitenancy as well. Detailed discussions on multitenancy is beyond the scope of this book.

Summary

We introduced various patterns of multitenancy. We discussed multitenancy in the context of Azure AD. We went through a demo application on how to leverage Azure's multitenancy to support an application's multitenant model.

We have covered authentication through the course of this book. We discussed how Azure AD can be integrated to support various authentication scenarios. In the last chapter, we touch on authorization and how can we use Azure AD for it.

CHAPTER 9

Introduction to Authorization

Throughout this book, we have discussed authentication and the process of authenticating users for different scenarios. We talked about authenticating users in different types of applications and through various types of providers. Authentication deals with identifying who the user is. It provides the user an identity and determines if the user can access the application. An application might want to restrict what a user can do within the application. This process of defining the permissions that a user has is called *authorization*. Whereas authentication deals with the *who*, authorization deals with the *what*.

Permissions can be determined on various criteria, such as the roles that have been assigned to the user, whether the user belongs to a certain organization, and so forth. We must be aware of the identity of the user in scenarios like these. To be provided specific permissions or authorization, the user must be authenticated and their identity must be established. Authorization can be at granularized at two levels.

- **Data**. Identifies which type or subset of data that the user can access. For example, in a multitenancy scenario, a user should only see data related to their organization.

© Manas Mayank and Mohit Garg 2019

M. Mayank and M. Garg, *Developing Applications with Azure Active Directory*,
https://doi.org/10.1007/978-1-4842-5040-2_9

- **Application**. Defines which specific features or parts of the application that a user has valid access to. Also defines which operations (i.e., create, read, update, delete) a user with access can do.

This chapter introduces the concepts of authorization. A detailed design of an application's authorization framework is dependent on the requirements of the application, which is beyond the scope of this book. We will discuss the following authorization mechanisms.

- Policy-based authorization

- Role-based authorization

- Security groups

- Claims-based authorization

- Resource-based authorization

Let's start by setting up our solution.

Setting up a Solution

Create a new project using the MVC template from Chapter 7. Ensure that you change the authentication to "Work or School Accounts" and check the "Read directory data" option (see Figure 9-1).

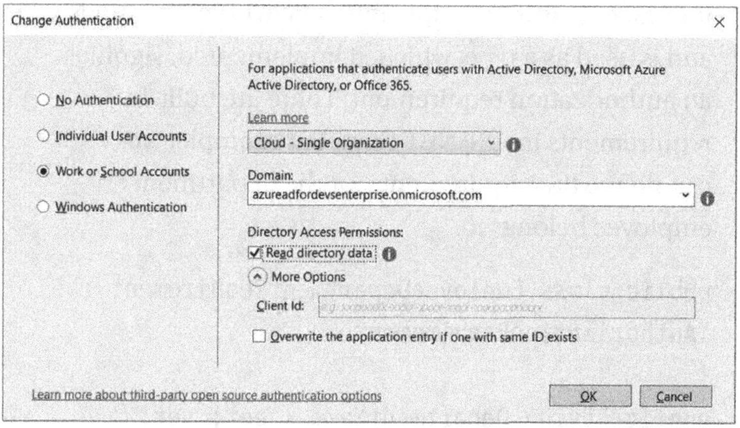

Figure 9-1. *Adding authentication during project creation*

Add a reference to OpenID Connect and ADAL-related libraries. We are using only the MVC web application to learn about the concepts of authorization. The same concepts could be extended for API controllers. We are using the same Azure AD tenant—azureadfordevsenterprise. onmicrosoft.com—in the examples. Confirm that the application is registered in Azure AD tenant. Let's start learning the concepts and creating our demo applications.

Policy-Based Authorization

ASP.NET Core provides abstraction for authorization mechanisms through policies. Policies are extendible and can be used with different authorization schemes. They decouple authorization from the controllers. Policies are based primarily on three types.

- **Requirement**. Encapsulates the data required for an authorization rule. The user identity is validated against the data parameters of a requirement. A requirement must implement the IAuthorizationRequirement

interface. This is an empty interface with no methods
and is used as a type, which, if implemented, signifies
an authorization requirement. There are built-in
requirements in ASP.NET Core. For example, we
can define the requirements for the department an
employee belongs to.

```
public class EmployeeDepartmentRequirement :
IAuthorizationRequirement
{
public string DepartmentName { get; set; }

public EmployeeDepartmentRequirement(string
departmentName)
{
this.DepartmentName = departmentName;
}
}
```

- **AuthorizationPolicy**. Signifies the policy that needs
  to be evaluated. A policy is a basic building block
  for authorization rules. It can have one or more
  requirements associated with it. All the requirements
  associated with a policy must succeed for a policy to
  succeed. Policies are added in ConfigureServices in
  Startup.cs. For example, we might want to have a policy
  specific to the HR admin. We will use the requirement
  we defined earlier and check if the user has the role of
  an admin. Let's name our policy HRAdminPolicy.

```
services.AddAuthorization(options =>
{
options.AddPolicy("HRAdminPolicy", policy => policy.
Requirements.Add(new EmployeeDepartmentRequirement("HR")));
```

```
options.AddPolicy("HRAdminPolicy", policy => policy.
RequireRole("admin"));
});
```

Policies can be applied to a controller or a method.
The following shows how a policy could be applied
for our scenario.

```
[Authorize(Policy = "HRAdminPolicy")]
public class HRAdminOperationsController : Controller
{
}
```

- **AuthorizationHandler**. Evaluates if a requirement
  is successful or not. The logic for authorization is
  encapsulated within it. A requirement could have one
  or more handlers associated with it. An authorization
  handler should inherit from an abstract class (Authori
  zationHandler<TRequirement>), where TRequirement
  is the type of requirement this handler caters to. This
  class has a HandleRequirementAsync method that
  has to be overridden in your code and contains logic
  to validate the requirement. In our scenario, we can
  define handler as follows.

```
public class EmployeeDepartmentHandler : Authorization
Handler<EmployeeDepartmentRequirement>
    {
        protected override Task HandleRequirementA
        sync(AuthorizationHandlerContext context,
        EmployeeDepartmentRequirement requirement)
        {
```

```
// Logic to check the department of the employee. For
// time being we will just let this requirement succeed.
context.Succeed(requirement);
                return Task.CompletedTask;
        }
    }
```

The handler must be registered in ConfigureServices method of Startup.cs.

```
services.AddSingleton<IAuthorizationHandler,
EmployeeDepartmentHandler>();
```

Policy-based authorization can be used with other authorization mechanisms. It forms the basis for all the other mechanisms that we discuss this chapter.

Role-Based Authorization

Role-based authorization has been used since legacy applications. Users can have a specific role assigned to them. The actions define the role needed to access them. For example, a user could belong to either an admin or an employee role. Some controllers allow access to users in an admin role. Traditionally, we check whether the user is assigned the specific role needed to access a controller. We will use policies for checking a user role. Let's start by defining the valid roles for our application and assigning the admin role to the user we created earlier: Enterprise User (enterpriseuser@azureadfordevsenterprise.onmicrosoft.com).

1. Go to your enterprise Azure AD tenant (azureadfordevsenterprise.onmicrosoft.com) in the Azure portal.

2. Go to "App registrations" and under the Manage menu, click Manifest. Click the same. This displays metadata for the application in JSON format.

3. Locate the appRoles element, change the value as follows, and save.

```
"appRoles": [
        {
                    "allowedMemberTypes": [
                            "User"
                    ],
                    "description": "Administrators ",
                    "displayName":
                    "Administrators",
                    "id": "68e9f85b-d6ab-4894-aae7-
                    483307986d26",
                    "isEnabled": true,
                    "lang": null,
                    "origin": "Application",
                    "value": "admin"
        },
        {

                    "allowedMemberTypes": [
                            "User"
                    ],
                    "description": "Employees",
                    "displayName": "Employees",
                    "id": "e6729ca2-e876-466d-aecb-
                    1b9c6a24de47",
                    "isEnabled": true,
                    "lang": null,
```

```
                              "origin": "Application",
                              "value": "employee"
                 }
          ]
```

This basically adds two roles to our application: admin and employee.

4. Go to Enterprise applications ➤ All applications and locate the application that you registered earlier in this chapter (AuthorizationDemo) and click it.

5. Go to "Users and groups" under Manage and click the checkbox in front of Enterprise User. Click the Edit button. This loads the Edit Assignment blade.

6. Choose Select Role to load the Select Role blade. This shows the two roles that you just added in the manifest.

Edit Assignment
Azure AD for Devs Enterprise

Users and groups
1 user selected.

Select Role
None Selected

🔎 Enter role name to filter items...

Administrators

Employees

Figure 9-2. *Assigning an app role to user*

7. Select the Administrators option, click the Select button, and then click the Assign button. This adds the role to the user of the application.

8. Go to Visual Studio. Put a breakpoint on the OnAuthorizationCodeReceived method of the OpenID Connect configuration class. Run your solution.

9. Check the claims on the ClaimsPrincipal of the context. You will find admin in the role claim. This allows the policy to succeed, and the user is authorized.

Figure 9-3. *Role claim for the user*

Security Groups

In the previous section, we gave a role explicitly to the user. Providing each user role explicitly could be quite cumbersome. As with other security systems, we can define security groups and add users to relevant security groups. We can then provide appropriate roles to these security groups. Let's start by defining the security groups for our system and then make changes in our code to honor this. We will have two security groups: AdminGroup and EmployeeGroup.

1. In the Azure portal, go to Groups ➤ All groups and click the "New group" button. This opens the "New group" blade.

2. Enter the relevant details for AdminGroup and click Create. Be sure to add the enterprise user as a member. Change the admin role to an employee role. This is necessary to validate that the user is given a role due to being part of a group rather than the role being assigned explicitly.

Figure 9-4. *Create security group*

3. Copy the object ID of the group created. Refer to
    Figure 9-5. We will use this later in our code.

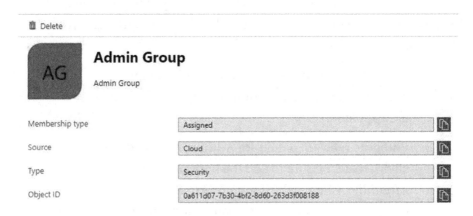

Figure 9-5. *Object ID for security group*

4. Create another group for employees and add users.
    Copy the object ID for this group as well.

5. Go to "App registrations" and under the Manage
    menu, click Manifest. On the manifest, locate the
    groupMembershipClaims element to SecurityGroup
    and save. This makes the security group part of the
    user claims.

    ```
    "groupMembershipClaims": "SecurityGroup"
    ```

6. Go to Visual Studio and locate the Startup.cs
    class. Under the ConfigureServices method, add
    an authorization policy for the security group, as
    follows.

    ```
    services.AddAuthorization(options =>
            {
                    options.AddPolicy("AdminGroupPolicy",
                    policy => policy.RequireClaim("groups",
                    "0a611d07-7b30-4bf2-8d60-
                    263d3f008188"));
            });
    ```

    The GUID in the code is the object ID for the group
    we created earlier. In the actual code, this GUID
    should be fetched from another mechanism.
    For example, you might get it from the Graph
    API or store it in a database table or in another
    configuration.

7. Go to Visual Studio. Put a breakpoint on the
    OnAuthorizationCodeReceived method of the
    OpenID Connect configuration class.

8. Add the policy to your HomeController and run the code.

```
[Authorize(Policy = "AdminGroupPolicy")]
public class HomeController : Controller
{
    ...
}
```

9. Check the claims on the ClaimsPrincipal of the
    context. The object ID for the admin security group
    is in the groups claim. This allows the policy to
    succeed, and the user is authorized.

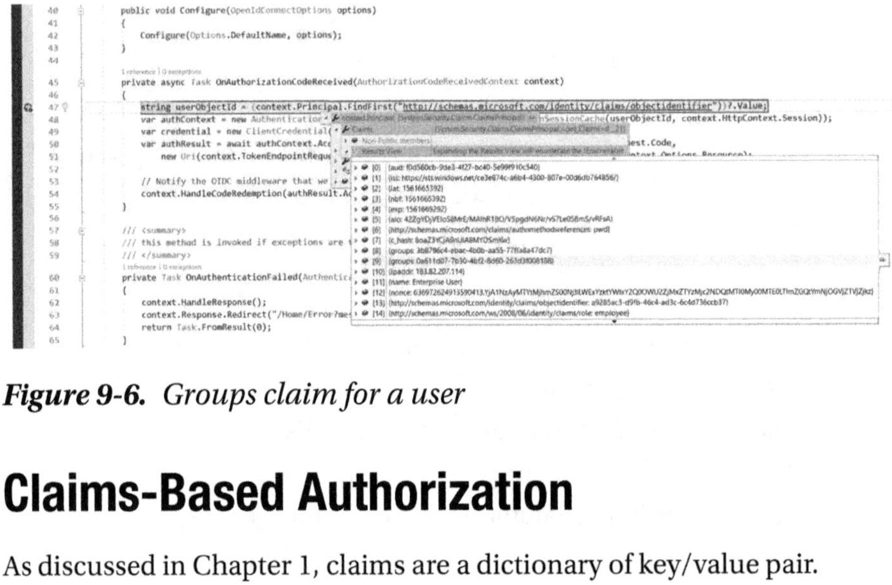

Figure 9-6. *Groups claim for a user*

Claims-Based Authorization

As discussed in Chapter 1, claims are a dictionary of key/value pair.
The claims are associated with an identity and provide information
relevant to the identity. Some of the claims are added by the identity
provider authenticating the user. Application code could also add claims
to an identity. This set of claims could be added in an application using
external storage, like a database or Azure AD itself. We can then make
authorization decisions based on the claims the user's identity has.

Let's start tweaking our code to validate claims. We will continue with the same example of validating an administrator for HR operations and check if our user has a claim for the HR department.

1. Go back to the Visual Studio solution and find our code with OpenID Connect configurations. Add the event handler to OIDC options.

```
options.Events.OnTokenValidated = TokenValidated;
```

2. Add the following code in the TokenValidated event handler. This event is raised as soon as the user's identity is established and validated.

```
private async Task TokenValidated(TokenValidatedContext
context)
        {
            string claimKey = "DepartmentClaim";
            // This value of the claim could be fetched
            // from from external storage like
            // database, depending on user's identity
            string claimValue = "HR";
            var claimsList = new List<Claim>
            {
                new Claim("DepartmentClaim", "HR")
            };
            var claimsIdentity = new ClaimsIdentity
            (claimsList);
            context.Principal.AddIdentity
            (claimsIdentity);
        }
```

For simplicity, we are just adding a hard-coded claim. In most scenarios, the user claim (e.g., a department) could be fetched from an external data source, like a database. This mapping of a department with a user can be maintained using the user's ObjectId (which is fetched from context.User).

3. It is time to add the missing logic to our requirement handler, EmployeeDepartmentHandler. Change the HandleRequirementAsync method.

```
protected override Task HandleRequirementA
sync(AuthorizationHandlerContext context,
EmployeeDepartmentRequirement requirement)
        {
            // Logic to check the department of the
            // employee
            if (context.User.
            HasClaim("DepartmentClaim", requirement.
            DepartmentName))
            {
                context.Succeed(requirement);
            }
            return Task.CompletedTask;
        }
```

4. Check that the department name in the user's claim is the same as the one specified during the policy setup (HR in our scenario). The policy succeeds, and the user is authorized. Put in a debug breakpoint and verify the claims.

Figure 9-7. *Claims validation for the user*

Customizing Azure AD Claims

In Chapter 6, you saw how to extend the schema of objects in Azure AD.
We also used Microsoft Graph. We can use the same principle to attach
the department name property to a user object in Azure AD. But we will
use an older version of Microsoft Graph called the Graph API, which is
still supported. This will also give us exposure to the Graph API. Let's go
through the steps. This is done using the Graph API described in previous
chapters. To simplify, we will use Azure AD Graph Explorer. This website
allows us to make Graph API requests through its interface.

1. Go to the manifest of your application in the Azure
   portal and note the ID element. This element is the
   object ID of the application (not the application or
   client ID).

2. Go to https://graphexplorer.azurewebsites.net/
   and log in with the admin of your enterprise Azure AD
   tenant. Note that this website does not work with live
   credentials (MSA) at the time of writing this book.

3. In the query textbox, enter the URL in the following
    format.

    https://graph.windows.net/<tenant-name>/
    applications/<application-objectid>/
    extensionProperties, where <tenant-name>
    is the name of your enterprise Azure tenant and
    <application-objectid> is the ID we noted in step 1.

4. Ensure that the request made is POST by changing
    the drop-down (see Figure 9-9). The text area
    under the query is enabled for a POST request.
    Add the following JSON there. The JSON simply
    indicates that we need to define a property called
    employeeDepartment of type String on the User
    object in the application's context.

```
{
    "name": "employeeDepartment",
    "dataType": "String",
    "targetObjects": [
        "User"
    ]
}
```

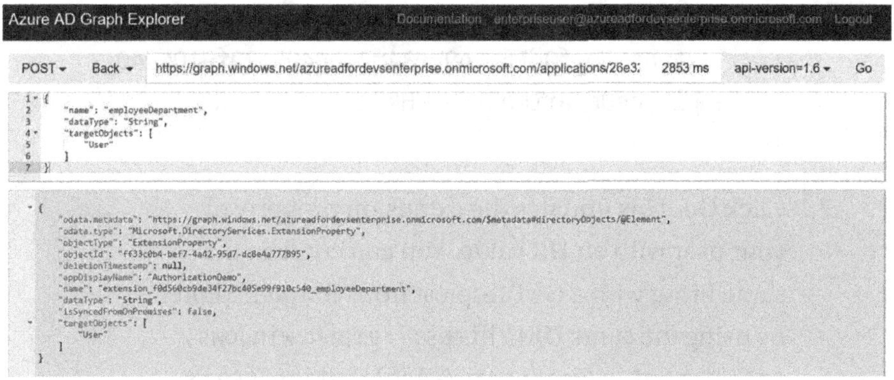

Figure 9-8. *Graph explorer: adding extension property*

5.   Click the Go button. This will send the Graph API request. If the request is successful, you will receive a JSON response, as shown in Figure 9-8. Pay attention to the name element in the response. Let's save it; we will be using it later.

```
"name": "extension_f0d560cb9de34f27bc405e99f910c540_
employeeDepartment"
```

6.   We need to assign a value to the extension property that we just added. Let's do it for our enterprise user. In Graph Explorer, change the query to update the extension property for your user:

```
https://graph.windows.net/<tenant-name>/
users/<application-user>
```
, where <application-user> is the fully qualified name of the user. Change the request type to PATCH from the drop-down menu and enter the following JSON for your request.

```
{
    "extension_f0d560cb9de34f27bc405e99f910c540_
    employeeDepartment": "HR"
}
```

7. Click Go. This updates the extension property of your user with an HR value. You can confirm the same firing with a GET request from Graph Explorer by using the same URL: `https://graph.windows.net/<tenant-name>/users/<application-user>`.

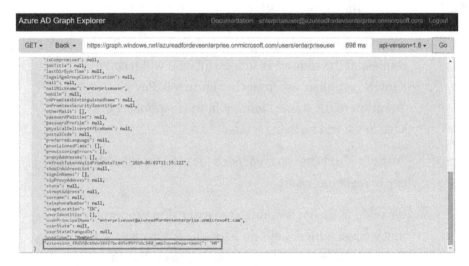

Figure 9-9. *Graph Explorer: getting user details*

In an actual application, this must be done either through PowerShell or code using the Graph API.

8. We now need to add this extension property as a claim. Go to the manifest of your application in the Azure portal and locate the optionalClaims element. Set the value for the same, as follows.

```
"optionalClaims": {
"idToken": [
{
"name": "extension_f0d560cb9de34f27bc405e99f910c540_
employeeDepartment",
"source": "user"
}
]
```

This basically tells your ID token to fetch the value of the extension property depicted by the name attribute defined on the user object's instance.

9. Go back to your Visual Studio solution and change the name of the claim to extn.employeeDepartment; this is the claim that will be populated.

10. protected override Task HandleRequirement Async(AuthorizationHandlerContext context, EmployeeDepartmentRequirement requirement)

```
{
    // Logic to check the department of the employee
    if (context.User.HasClaim("extn.
    employeeDepartment", requirement.DepartmentName))
    {
        context.Succeed(requirement);
    }

    return Task.CompletedTask;
}
```

11. Remove the TokenValidated event handler because the claim is already added.

12. Run your solution after putting a debug breakpoint on the method that we tweaked earlier. The claim is populated for the relevant user.

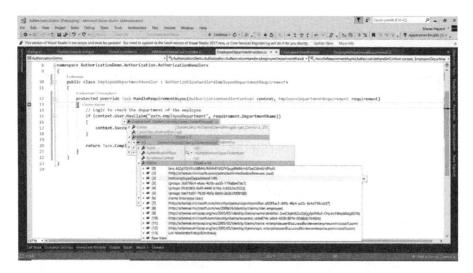

Figure 9-10.   *Claims using extension property*

Resource-based Authorization

At times, the authorization strategy depends on the resource itself. The resource being accessed defines the permissions needed to execute a particular action on it. We need to check if the user trying to perform an action on the resource has those permissions. If the user does have those permissions, we allow the user to perform the action; otherwise, we deny the action. Let's look at an example. We will extend the example we discussed in the previous section. Assume an organization needs to define authorization on HR department–related operations on employee records. The user could either read or write (edit) these records. The following are the requirements.

- Any employee can see her or his own employee record.

- Only an HR employee can see the records of other employees; other employees can't see these records.

- No employee can edit an employee record.

We will use the policy-based authorization here as well. We will mock the data where needed. Let's start by defining our requirement.

```
public class ResourcePermissionsRequirement :
IAuthorizationRequirement
    {
        public string Resource { get; set; }
        public string Permission { get; set; }

        public ResourcePermissionsRequirement(string resource,
        string permission)
        {
            this.Resource = resource;
            this.Permission = permission;
        }
    }
```

The requirement has two properties.

- **Resource**. Defines the resource being accessed. In our case, it could be defined as HROperations.

- **Permission**. Defines a valid permission in the resource. Permissions could simply be defined as create, read, update, or delete. We will use read or write as our valid permissions. This implies that a user can either read or write to HROperations.

Let's define policies for read and write in Startup.cs.

```
services.AddAuthorization(options =>
        {
            options.AddPolicy("HROperationsReadPolicy",
            policy => policy.Requirements.Add(new Reso
            urcePermissionsRequirement("HROperations",
            "read")));
            options.AddPolicy("HROperationsWritePolicy",
            policy => policy.Requirements.Add(new Reso
            urcePermissionsRequirement("HROperations",
            "write")));
        });
```

Define the entity that encapsulates the employee record. Properties are self-explanatory.

```
public class EmployeeEntity
    {
        public int EmployeeId { get; set; }
        public string EmployeeName { get; set; }
        public string Department { get; set; }
        public string Designation { get; set; }
    }
```

Let's define the handler, which accepts an entity as well. This is done by making the handler inherit from AuthorizationHandler<TRequirement, TEntity>, where TRequirement is the requirement on which the handler is applicable, and TEntity is the type of entity on which an operation is being done.

```
public class ResourcePermissionsHandler :
        AuthorizationHandler<ResourcePermissionsRequirement,
        EmployeeEntity>
```

```
{
    protected override Task HandleRequirementA
    sync(AuthorizationHandlerContext context,
    ResourcePermissionsRequirement requirement,
    EmployeeEntity employee)
    {
        string employeeIdFromClaims = context.User.Claims.
        FirstOrDefault(c => c.Type == "EmployeeId").Value;
        if (context.User.HasClaim(requirement.Resource,
        requirement.Permission) || employee.EmployeeId.
        ToString() == employeeIdFromClaims)
        {
            context.Succeed(requirement);
        }

        return Task.CompletedTask;
    }
}
```

We authorize if the user has the right claims. We define our claim as a combination of resources and permissions. In addition to permissions on the resource, we check if the employee ID of the logged-in user (which we check through the EmployeeId claim) and the employee ID in the employee entity (or employee record being accessed) is the same. If either of the conditions match, we allow the authorization to succeed. Let's now look at how to invoke this handler.

Since our authorization strategy depends on the employee entity (as an instance of the EmployeeEntity class), we can't use policies through controller or method-level attributes. Hence, the attribute (like [Authorize(Policy = "HRAdminPolicy")], which we used previously) will not suffice for our requirements. The decision to authorize has to be taken in the controller code. ASP.NET Core uses the IAuthorizationService interface for authorization. This interface could be accessed through dependency injection in the controller. We can call the following method on this interface to execute our handler.

```
Task<AuthorizationResult> AuthorizeAsync(ClaimsPrincipal user,
object resource, string policyName);
```

Before we call this method, let's mock our employee record service. This service mocks an employee and returns an entity corresponding to the employee. For simplicity, assume that the HR employee has employee ID 1. The other IDs belong to other employees. We can define a simple mock employee service as follows.

```
public class MockEmployeeService : IMockEmployeeService
    {
        public EmployeeEntity CreateMockEmployee(int employeeId)
        {
            if (employeeId == 1)
            {
                return new EmployeeEntity() { Department =
                "HR", Designation = "Manager", EmployeeId = 1,
                EmployeeName = "HR Sharma" };
            }
            else
            {
                return new EmployeeEntity() { Department =
                "FINANCE", Designation = "Accountant", EmployeeId
                = employeeId, EmployeeName = "FI Nance" };
            }
        }
    }
```

Now we will try to authorize actions in the HRAdminOperationsController HR operations controller.

Register the types with a DI container in Startup.cs.

```
services.AddSingleton<IAuthorizationHandler,
ResourcePermissionsHandler>();
services.AddSingleton<IMockEmployeeService,
MockEmployeeService>();
```

Inject the relevant interfaces and assign them to the local variables.

```
private readonly IAuthorizationService authorizationService;
    private readonly IMockEmployeeService mockEmployeeService;

    public HRAdminOperationsController(IAuthorizationS
    ervice authorizationService, IMockEmployeeService
    mockEmployeeService)
    {
        this.authorizationService = authorizationService;
        this.mockEmployeeService = mockEmployeeService;
    }
```

Go to the Details method and tweak the code as follows.

```
public async Task<IActionResult> Details(int id)
    {
        EmployeeEntity employeeEntity = this.
        mockEmployeeService.CreateMockEmployee(id);
        var result = await this.authorizationService.
        AuthorizeAsync(this.User, employeeEntity,
        "HROperationsReadPolicy");
        if (result.Succeeded)
        {
            return View();
        }

        return Forbid();
    }
```

This is the method to read the employee records with the employee ID specified by the id parameter. If the policy passes, we authorize the request. Similarly, change the Edit-related controller as follows. The code is self-explanatory.

```
public async Task<IActionResult> Edit(int id)
        {
            EmployeeEntity = this.mockEmployeeService.
            CreateMockEmployee(id);
            var result = await this.authorizationService.
            AuthorizeAsync(this.User, employeeEntity,
            "HROperationsWritePolicy");
            if (result.Succeeded)
            {
                return View();
            }

            return Forbid();
        }
```

Let's also mock adding claims in the OpenID Connect configurations (ensure this method is added as an event handler for the OnTokenValidated event).

```
private async Task TokenValidated(TokenValidatedContext context)
        {
            ClaimsIdentity = null;

            if (context.Principal.HasClaim("extn.
            employeeDepartment", "HR"))
            {
                claimsIdentity = this.GetHREmployeeClaim();
            }
            else
```

```
    {
        claimsIdentity = this.GetOtherEmployeeClaim();
    }

    context.Principal.AddIdentity(claimsIdentity);
}

// Mock getting claims for HR employees
private ClaimsIdentity GetHREmployeeClaim()
{
    var claimsList = new List<Claim>
    {
        new Claim("DepartmentClaim", "HR"),
        new Claim("HROperations", "read"),
        new Claim("EmployeeId", "1")
    };
    var claimsIdentity = new ClaimsIdentity(claimsList);
    return claimsIdentity;
}

// Mock getting claims for non HR employees
private ClaimsIdentity GetOtherEmployeeClaim()
{
    var claimsList = new List<Claim>
    {
        new Claim("DepartmentClaim", "Finance"),
        new Claim("EmployeeId", "2")
    };
    var claimsIdentity = new ClaimsIdentity(claimsList);
    return claimsIdentity;
}
```

Let's identify if the employee is part of HR, which depends on the claim from the extension property we added in the claims-based authorization section.

Run the code and log in with the user having the extension property populated with the HR value (such as Enterprise User; we added the value for the extension property in the last section) and try to access the Edit controller by passing the ID as 1 (assumed to be HR) in the request and again with 2 as the ID. You will note that edit controller authorized in the first case but not in the second case. Try the same on the Details controllers for both combinations. In addition, try all the combinations with a non-HR user as well. The authorization logic works as expected.

Table 9-1. *For Getting the Details*

Operation	URL	Actor: HR	Actor: non-HR
Reading HR employee's record	<app-url>/ HRAdminOperations/ Details/1	Authorized	Not Authorized
Another employee's record reading	<app-url>/ HRAdminOperations/ Details/2	Authorized	Authorized

Table 9-2. *For the Editing Employee Records*

Operation	URL	Actor: HR	Actor: non-HR
Editing HR employee's record	<app-url>/ HRAdminOperations/ Edit/1	Authorized	Not Authorized
Another employee's record editing	<app-url>/ HRAdminOperations/ Edit/2	Not Authorized	Authorized

274

We can extend this resource-based authorization to other resources. This combination of resources and permissions provides a powerful and extendible mechanism for authorization.

Summary

In this chapter, we introduced how to integrate your Azure AD–based application with authorization. The concepts we discussed are relevant to other identity providers as well. We discussed various mechanisms to implement authorization. The choice of authorization should depend on the actual application requirements. A complex authorization strategy for a simplistic application requirement will add unnecessary complications. The opposite is true as well.

Index

Printed in the United States
By Bookmasters